Supporting
Early Literacies
through Play

Sara Miller McCune founded SAGE Publishing in 1965 to support the dissemination of usable knowledge and educate a global community. SAGE publishes more than 1000 journals and over 800 new books each year, spanning a wide range of subject areas. Our growing selection of library products includes archives, data, case studies and video. SAGE remains majority owned by our founder and after her lifetime will become owned by a charitable trust that secures the company's continued independence.

Los Angeles | London | New Delhi | Singapore | Washington DC | Melbourne

Supporting
Early Literacies
through Play

Kate Smith & Karen Vincent

Los Angeles | London | New Delhi
Singapore | Washington DC | Melbourne

Los Angeles | London | New Delhi
Singapore | Washington DC | Melbourne

SAGE Publications Ltd
1 Oliver's Yard
55 City Road
London EC1Y 1SP

SAGE Publications Inc.
2455 Teller Road
Thousand Oaks, California 91320

SAGE Publications India Pvt Ltd
B 1/I 1 Mohan Cooperative Industrial Area
Mathura Road
New Delhi 110 044

SAGE Publications Asia-Pacific Pte Ltd
3 Church Street
#10-04 Samsung Hub
Singapore 049483

Editor: Delayna Spencer
Assistant editor: Catriona McMullen
Production editor: Jessica Masih
Copyeditor: Clare Weaver
Proofreader: Jill Birch
Indexer: Elske Janssen
Marketing manager: Dilhara Attygalle
Cover design: Wendy Scott
Typeset by KnowledgeWorks Global Ltd.
Printed in the UK

Library of Congress Control Number: 2021936752

British Library Cataloguing in Publication data

A catalogue record for this book is available from the
British Library

ISBN 978-1-5264-8739-1
ISBN 978-1-5264-8738-4 (pbk)

At SAGE we take sustainability seriously. Most of our products are printed in the UK using responsibly
sourced papers and boards. When we print overseas we ensure sustainable papers are used as measured
by the PREPS grading system. We undertake an annual audit to monitor our sustainability.

CONTENTS

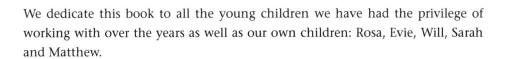

We dedicate this book to all the young children we have had the privilege of working with over the years as well as our own children: Rosa, Evie, Will, Sarah and Matthew.

Thank you for sharing the brilliance of play with us.

ABOUT THE AUTHORS

Kate Smith is a Senior Lecturer in Childhood and Early Childhood Studies at Canterbury Christ Church University. She currently leads modules on language and literacy and supervises post-graduate and research students. As a Senior Fellow of the Higher Education Academy she has led employment-based under-graduate programmes and travelled to Sweden, Finland and Norway as part of her university role. Kate's PhD used participatory methodology to explore young children's mark-making and writing in their first year of school. She continues to research young children's literacies and has published a number of articles. Before lecturing she was a primary teacher working with children aged 3–7 in London and Kent schools with whole-school responsibility for Literacy and Art. Kate's work with schools continues in her role as a Director of a Multi Academy Trust in Kent. She is co-editor of *An Introduction to Early Childhood* (2018) and has recently contributed to the *Birth to Five Matters* documentation. She is a member of EECERA, UKLA and BERA.

Karen Vincent is a Senior Lecturer in Early Childhood and Primary Initial Teacher Education. She is a Senior Fellow of the Higher Education Academy and is the Primary Lead for Early Years at Canterbury Christ Church University. She currently leads the early childhood placement modules, teaches modules on child development and learning and supervises final year research students. Karen's doctoral thesis explores the pedagogical narratives of early childhood initial teacher educators. As a teacher of young children, Karen taught in a range of dif-ferent school settings in a variety of leadership roles, before becoming a teacher educator. Karen has written several chapters and articles relating to early years and primary initial teacher education. These include pedagogies of play, play and mathematics, literacy transition from EYFS to KS1 and mentoring. Karen is a member of IPDA, TACTYC and The Chartered College of Teaching.

INTRODUCTION: WEAVING TOGETHER YOUNG CHILDREN'S PLAY AND LITERACIES

Within our personal and professional lives we have been privileged to have had many opportunities to observe and reflect on the joyful inventiveness of young children's play. What has become apparent through careful noticing over time are the important connections that exist between play and literacy and the possibilities that play offers young children in becoming adaptable, dexterous and imaginative literacy users. These arguments, that children's literacy skills and knowledge can be effectively developed through play activity, particularly symbolic and pretend play, are already well established in literature (Pellegrini, 1985; Hall and Robinson, 2003; Roskos and Christie, 2011; Christie and Roskos, 2013; Wohlwend, 2018). The aim of this book is to explore these ideas by bringing together research and theory that helps us understand this pivotal relationship and demonstrate why children's play should be prioritised in supporting their engagement with literacies.

This book will introduce you to both traditional theories of play, language and literacy as well as more contemporary understandings of literacies. We highlight the significance of the pioneers of play, whose ideas still resonate with us in the values we attribute to play as well as in the day-to-day learning practices in early years settings, and also bring to the fore more recent considerations that surround early childhood play as a more-than-human activity, one that is hybrid and relational in nature. This examination of play, one that combines the philosophical underpinnings of explorative play as learning with the more-than-human connective qualities of its action, will enhance your understanding of how to support diverse and inclusive literacies for all children.

The literate world today is plural and diverse – not one literacy exists but multiple literacies, and this is why play is such a useful device in literacy learning as it provides children with multiple ways of being and becoming with different literacies. A multiliteracies approach, one where children are encouraged to play with texts that are both linear (e.g. reading and writing) as well as non-linear (e.g. visual design, film and audio), is increasingly necessary so that children have the diverse skills and knowledge needed to actively produce and read a variety of texts that they encounter in everyday life (Cope and Kalantzis, 2000). Literacies exist in a range of spaces and places that children move between; young children are learning to adjust, select and practise different aspects of literacy dependent on the social and material context they are in (Kalantzis and Cope,

2008). As we will show in the pages ahead, the fluidity of play aids this flexibility by encouraging children to adjust and transform literacy in response to their environment.

Playing… learning… being playful

The United Nations Convention on the Rights of Children (UNICEF, 1989) states that every child must be free to express their thoughts and opinions (Article 13) and be able to share their views, feelings and wishes in all matters affecting them (Article 12). We believe that play, also an essential right for children (Article 31), enables children's freedom of expression and participation, and can effect change in very powerful ways if listened to effectively. Play provides a means for children to use their bodies in multimodal ways to show their thinking and interests, to have their 'say' and express who they are. In this way, play can be viewed as activism, a powerful way for children to exert themselves in a society where their exertions are often overlooked.

> Play – and its affective, interactive, and subjunctive characteristics – can provide a counterpoint to cynicism engendered in a world where actions seem futile or are co-opted before even being realised. There is always an alternative in play. As a slightly more liminal and less existentially fraught space, play allows for experimentation, creation, as well as imagining and enacting new ways of being and living. (Rosen, 2017, pp. 118–119)

Adults who support young children's literacies are often positioned powerfully as interpreters of the meanings and purposes of young children's play – these diverse perspectives are presented throughout the following chapters. However, the message in this book that we hope is loud and clear, is that the meanings of play are essentially understood and expressed by children, not adults. To fully make sense of the complexities and opportunities that exist in children's play we must respect children's authority and expertise as play makers as a starting point for close observation. Young children value play as a means to exercise autonomy and pursue their own interests with friends (Howe, 2016). They also understand how learning and play are connected through what the educator does; the adult 'presence' and the play spaces they make available (Pyle and Alaca, 2018). Adults, therefore, have a significant influence on how children perceive their play – the values that are attached to it.

The success of children's literacy play relies on the selection of materials, the time made available, the stimulus and provocations introduced, the language used to extend thinking and imagination, and the skills and experiences of different literacies that are shared. Equally important are the relationships that are formed between educators and carers and children, the trust that adults have in children's self-initiated play, their abilities to listen with care and, importantly, to enjoy the reciprocity of playful literacy learning. These adult–child collaborations, or play partnerships, are important elements in building meaningful literacy encounters. You will be invited in the chapters ahead to consider your own role in creating playful opportunities that extend children's literacies and hopefully recognise how your actions have great importance in children's literacy learning.

Early literacy: A social justice imperative

Providing meaningful opportunities for literacy play at a young age is a matter of social justice. We know that poorer children in society have lower attainment in literacy as they move through the education system (EEF, 2018a) and that these inequalities in achievement are not improving (Hutchinson et al., 2019). For years, third sector and educational organisations as well as government agencies have written about the importance of 'closing the gap' in language and literacy within the early years to avoid children falling behind in their later reading and writing (Roulstone et al., 2011; Tickell, 2011; Save the Children, 2015; EEF, 2018b).

We have concerns about the tendency towards reductive models of literacy, as well as the deficit constructions of young children who need 'future-proofing' contained in some of these publications. Inequalities exist in the social and material environments that young children experience that unjustly affects their opportunities to engage with different types of literacy. However, a quick fix in the form of an early intervention or a narrowing of the types of literacy on offer will not suffice in closing and sustaining measurable gaps in knowledge when there are complex macro and micro level factors that affect children's language and literacy learning. More work needs to be carried out with educators to identify how best to support socially and economically disadvantaged children and their families with resources available to extend children's diverse range of literacy knowledge, rather than limit it to what is easily measured. This book has been written to highlight a range of activities that can make a real difference in supporting all children to be active, experimental and adept literacy users and makers.

The chapters ahead: Creating a dialogue

As educators we have learnt about play and literacies from children, but we also owe a great debt to our academic colleagues, particularly Professors Kathy Goouch and Sacha Powell, who have advocated so fiercely in their work for the importance of early relationships as a foundation for literacy and the expertise that babies and toddlers have (Goouch and Powell, 2013). Within these pages, we hope in our small way to continue the valuable conversations we have had with colleagues, students, educators and carers over the years. We encourage you as a reader to join in with this dialogue by critically engaging with the theory and practice presented in order to extend your own ideas in supporting young children's literacies.

The first two chapters in the book lay the foundations for learning literacies through play. Chapter 1 focuses specifically on play, introducing you to key writers in the field from the past (e.g. Froebel and Dewey) as well as debates about play in contemporary academia and practice. Chapter 2 explores the broad notion of language as a foundation for literacy and the social and environmental factors, particularly close relationships, that support young children's participation as language users and literacy makers. The following five chapters look at different modes of text making: storytelling, writing and reading as well as different literacy spaces: digital and outdoor. Although each of these elements of literacy have been examined separately, they are overlapping and we advocate a hybrid approach to these in play so that children can bring different literacies together. Other modes of literacy that are mentioned, for example touch, sound, visual texts, are equally important and we hope that you are able to identify links with diverse forms of literacy throughout the book. To illustrate the content of each chapter, you will be presented with vignettes of children playing, case studies of practice, reflective questions, pedagogical questions to prompt discussion with others, ideas for practice and recommendations for further reading. The final chapter of the book focuses specifically on how play and literacies are understood within different curriculum frameworks to help you identify what works best in planning for and assessing high-quality and playful literacies.

And finally, before you delve in

Young children have both an entitlement to play (Moyles, 2014) and a human right to literacy (Flewitt, 2013). For those who have a responsibility to educate our youngest children it is important to recognise that young children's play is their learning. Following the logic of this, young children's play *is* their literacy learning. This book has been written not only as an explanation of how play supports diverse literacies but also as a petition for taking play seriously as learning within early years settings. Young children's play shouldn't need a plea of defence, or a promotional marketing campaign; however, we are increasingly aware that in the current educational climate, play is under considerable pressure to 'perform', particularly in English classrooms (TACTYC, 2017). Tensions exist between the formal teaching of literacy knowledge, for example phonics, and a child's right to play. Young children's play, as process-driven, self-directed, and freely chosen activity, is essentially nebulous and unpredictable. Literacy learning interpreted as outcome orientated and fixed to linear goals does not fit well with this. However, if it is the prism of assessment and accountability that causes a separation between play and literacy, then this isn't a problem of playful literacies (and all that it can offer), but of an external system of quantifying learning that needs to be challenged. Phonics can be taught in a playful, child-initiated and exploratory way; if testing children narrows these possibilities then we are narrowing the literacies that we offer young children, a counter-intuitive approach to literacy education.

Play as a heterogeneous affair with multiple paths and endings is what makes it so important for learning about literacies. It offers a space for exploring the materials, symbols, and purpose of literacies in expansive ways. We hope that this book helps you in becoming an advocate for play as an ideal space through which young children can build knowledge of the multitude of literacies that exist as part of every-day life and from this, a love for literacy learning.

1

STRONG FOUNDATIONS: THE SIGNIFICANCE OF PLAY

This chapter will

- introduce you to the ideas of Froebel, Montessori, Dewey, Issacs, Malaguzzi and show how these theories underpin play practices in early years settings and schools;
- highlight the different types, categories and forms of play;
- help you to identify some of the challenges of organising play as a pedagogical tool;
- encourage you to consider the role that adults have in children's play;
- familiarise you with more recent theories of play.

Young children have the capacity to play in multiple ways, with multiple things, and in multiple spaces. Play is complex, messy, transformational and, due to its shifting meanings, very difficult to define (Sutton-Smith, 1997). It is also contradictory, involving risk and subversion, as well as rules and repetition. Play activity can entail trying to reach a goal but can also be an exploration with no outcomes in mind. Acknowledging that play is ambiguous and sometimes paradoxical, however, is not the end of the story. We still need to recognise that observing the features of play helps us to create the best possible pedagogical approach, particularly one that supports young children's literacies.

This chapter provides a broad overview of the different theories and approaches to play that help us in understanding children's play practices. The chapter begins with an overview of influential play philosophers, recognising the value that educationalists have given to play as not only a vehicle for learning, but also a way of being in and with the world. The theorists presented for discussion all emphasise different functions and features of play, helping us to recognise the different ways in which educators engage children in learning through play (Moyles, 2010) and therefore the most effective way of supporting and extending learning in young children through playful pedagogies.

To get you thinking about some of the ideas that will be presented, the following vignette shows how two young children are experiencing play as a way of being in and with the world. They are appropriating natural materials and shaping them to suit their play desires. You can see how they are learning to manipulate the natural materials, work alongside and respond to each other and to adjust their behaviour to achieve their desired goals.

Vignette

Explorative play with bodies and materials

It is a warm, Spring day in April. Ben (aged 3) is with his sister Lucy (aged 5) at a local park that has a huge sandpit. The sandpit is surrounded by several trees and branches that have been broken off by the recent strong winds. The windswept branches lie in the surrounding area of the sandpit. Today, the wind has died down and the sun has emerged to warm the sand. Ben and Lucy run straight to the sandpit and after a while exploring their footprints in the sand and experiencing the sensation of walking on a surface that offers more resistance than usual, Ben follows his sister to the edge of the sandpit. He watches as she grabs a branch and begins to snap off the side pieces. 'I need a stick' she declares before taking it back into the sandpit waving it for all to see. In response, Ben moves towards a tree and begins to look for his own branch, selecting one nearby. He bends down to pick it up and takes it over to show his sister. 'Do you want a stick too?' she asks. Ben nods and she takes it from him and snaps off the small side branches before handing it back to him and continuing to use her stick to 'dig' in the sand. Ben takes his cue and too begins to 'dig' in the sand, rubbing his face gently when the sand flicks upwards. In response to the gritty sensation of the sand on his face, he changes the orientation of his stick so that the sand flies in a different direction. 'I'm making a hole' he declares to his sister who responds by moving closer so that she can assist him in making his hole deeper and wider. After a few minutes of activity, Lucy moves back to her original hole nearby, kneels down on the soft sand and begins to poke her stick through the bottom of the hole in the direction of Ben's. Eventually, the end of her stick appears at the bottom of his hole. He giggles in delight and responds by pushing his stick into the newly created tunnel that connects their holes. Ben lies down on the sand so that he can reach his stick further into his hole, moving it up and down and side to side to push the sand away and create a bigger tunnel. Lucy runs over to her mother to ask for a tissue which she then pokes the stick through, before placing the 'flag' proudly into the sand on top of the tunnel.

You will see that the role of the adult in the above vignette was minimal but nevertheless important in providing a valuable resource at the right time! The following section will explore some of the key ideas and philosophical perspectives that have emerged from the work of the early pioneers of play that will help you to understand play as young children's learning and the important role that adults have in supporting learning as play.

Pioneers of play: philosophical underpinnings of a play curriculum

Friedrich Froebel (1782–1852)

Froebel was a German educational pioneer who was influenced by the Romantic philosophical movement of his time and educational thinkers he had worked alongside such as Johann Heinrich Pestalozzi (1746–1827). Froebel was particularly affected by Pestalozzi's approach to pedagogy where children were free to follow their natural interests and learn through self-activity rather than as a response to others (Brühlmeier, 2010). Froebel's work is still significant, principally in how it radically challenges our assumptions about childhood. Froebel viewed childhood as a meaningful chapter of human life starting shortly after birth, rather than as mere preparation for adulthood. His extensive writing, particularly *The Education of Man* (1887), provides us with in-depth observations of young children at play that accentuate how children are immersed in their own self-driven activities. The descriptions he presents to the reader value the moments of time when play activity occurs. Froebel highlighted the creative drive and curiosity inherent in children's play and concluded that play is,

> ... the highest expression of human development in childhood for it alone is the free expression of what is in the child's soul. (Froebel, 1826, trans. 1912)

A Froebelian approach to early childhood education is to begin by respecting the integrity of each child in their own right and to recognise the unique capacity and potential they have to express who they are through their play (Froebel Trust, 2019). However, pedagogical tensions can exist in this approach when applied to practices where play is viewed as a framework for learning, as for example in the EYFS (DfE, 2021). These frameworks, where adults organise and lead play, could be seen to weaken the value of genuine play that Froebel argued for, which is defined by the mastery and autonomy that young children derive when they initiate, create and lead play for themselves (Murray, 2018).

Since publication, Froebel's work has influenced ideas about how we organise provision for young children. He was committed to the idea that learning was a result of children's natural holistic development, where the physical, cognitive, social, emotional, and importantly the spiritual come together. Learning happens successfully through a child's self-activity where each aspect of their human experience can be nourished. His idea of education was one where the child's emerging unity with the world should be supported, and their naturally developing 'wholeness' preserved. So, applying a Froebelian approach to learning means connecting each aspect of a child's development. For Froebel, this holistic learning in young children can be observed in play where children create relationships with each other and the world (Bruce, 2012).

As a deeply religious man, Froebel believed that the purpose of education was to help an individual to develop a harmony between themselves, nature and God. Therefore, the natural environment was an integral part of a child's early education. Froebel founded a number of 'kindergartens', translated as 'gardens for children', where children studied and cultivated nature in unison with practitioners who, in turn, tended to children as a gardener would nurture the plants in their care (Tovey, 2013).

Froebel developed pedagogical resources for mothers and women, who he thought were naturally placed to carry out this caring role. He created 'gifts' and 'occupations', a hands-on set of resources that adults could use with children. These objects and activities mirrored the physical forms and relationships found in nature and the mathematical and natural logic underlying all things natural. He also valued music, particularly singing, as a way of channelling emotional expression, publishing for example, *The Mother-Song Book* of 1844 which recommended singing to young children as a way of communicating feelings of love and care (Powell et al., 2013).

Froebel's ideas are significant today as they focus our attention on the importance of creating learning environments that stimulate children's natural desire to learn and do not repress a child's creative self-activity. His work is important for those of us who are interested in children's early literacies in that it values being 'present' with children in the precious moments when children are making and representing their ideas through gesture, speech or symbols, rather than focusing on external aims and objectives that may detract from this. His ideas also help us to consider language and literacy in terms of a child's wholeness; that when children are learning literacies, they do so through the unification of their body, mind and spirit. Finally, Froebel encourages us to value and enhance children's emotional literacy by recognising how play fosters love between the child and the parent and/or carer, as well as other children and the natural environment.

Reflection

What do you understand by the term holistic learning? What aspects of Froebel's philosophy of play do you think are most important?

Maria Montessori (1870–1952)

Maria Montessori studied as a medical doctor in Italy and applied her scientific training to her 'method' of educating young children. Her textbook, *The Montessori Method*, published in 1909 and first translated into English in 1912, prescribed the environment and activities that practitioners, known as directresses, needed to adopt. Montessori based her ideas on careful observations of children and advocated a detailed examination of what children are able to do as a starting point in developing a logical planning process to support children's individual learning. She argued that practitioners need to be aware of children's periods of sensitivity to learning – when they are ready to learn a new skill – so that they are able to introduce appropriate activities based on the child's abilities.

Montessori was influenced by Froebel's philosophy, valuing early education, particularly the role the environment and carers have in children's development. She argued that adults should encourage children to identify mathematical patterns from birth, linking with the notion that the main purpose of education is to create order and beauty within the environment. One of the most significant aspects of her ideas is that she allotted great value to children's independence and their play activity, famously describing it as 'a child's work'; equal in worth to any adult's productive occupation. The learning environment she advocated included scaled-down 'adult' objects, such as small tables and chairs and dustpan and brushes, designed to fit children's smaller bodies. These tools were not compromised in their value as they were made from the same materials and used in the same way as adults would use them.

The curriculum that Montessori espoused brought the physical, cognitive and material together through practical life skills that would help children become useful citizens of the world. Montessori argued that children have the capacity to choose resources for themselves and find their own ways to solve problems in how they use these tools. Encouraging children to 'do it themselves', she argued, is an important way for them to develop self-discipline and self-regulation. The resources children played with in her pedagogical approach, the puzzles and sensory task focused toys, sometimes with tiny pieces, supported this idea as they had to be ordered and carefully looked after.

The emphasis in Montessori's theory is on refining children's senses through play with real objects. Montessori argued, like Piaget (1971), that children's learning occurs as they move from the concrete (real) to the abstract, and that concrete experience needs to be carefully prepared by using resources that engage children's senses. For example, in today's Montessori settings the children would be encouraged to trace symbols with their fingers and play with moveable sandpaper letters. This physical activity where children can feel and explore the shape of letters is important for children to do before they use them in more abstract ways such as sounding them out, identifying them in other texts or writing them themselves. Children need to develop their motor skills in handling reading and writing tools before they can develop their intellectual engagement with them.

One of the most controversial aspects of Montessori's original approach was her discouragement of fantasy and imaginative play which she argued was a distraction from 'real' learning; she felt that children's time should be spent on more constructive 'real life' activities (Montessori, 1965). This reasoning led her to believe that a child's free drawings are 'nothing but monstrous expressions of intellectual lawlessness' (Montessori, 1918, p. 308). The Montessori approach to learning is still very popular worldwide and has been adopted by many early childhood settings. Over time, her ideas have been interpreted and adapted in different ways depending on the different contexts in which they are taught. Many settings now acknowledge and value children's imaginative abilities and are interpreting the Montessori philosophy of play and learning which emphasises a developmental, methodical, sensory-rich curriculum, into their own ways of working. The role of imagination in children's early literacy will be explored in further depth in Chapter 4.

John Dewey (1859–1952)

Dewey was an American philosopher who was interested in how education could be a means for creating inquiring and democratic citizens. His focus was on child-centred practical learning where the child's learning process, rather than the subject to be learnt, was central (Dewey, 2015 [1902]). He founded a short-lived experimental 'Laboratory School' (1896–1904) to test his notion that education could integrate learning with experience and a school could become a 'community of inquiry' (Durst, 2010). Like Froebel and Montessori, he was an advocate of children learning through experience, or hands-on education, interested in how this approach helps children to realise their potential and prepare them for a future life where they have 'command of themselves'.

In his writing, Dewey explored the relationship between play and work and how they were organised within the curriculum in schools at the time, claiming that these two interrelated activities should co-exist in the curriculum as both have serious intent for the learner (Skilbeck, 2017). He thought that children's play was a synchronisation of seriousness and playfulness – playfulness being an 'attitude of mind', whereas play being an expression or vehicle of the child's attitude.

Reflection

Do you agree with Dewey that play and playfulness are different? What do you think would be a good balance of work and play in an early years setting? How helpful is this distinction?

Dewey's ideas about the purpose of the curriculum and how the child and teacher come together in equal balance to form knowledge are still current in the language and debates that surround our approach to teaching young children about literacy. For example, the term 'sustained shared thinking' (Sylva et al., 2004) is prevalent in early years research, policy and rhetoric, as an indicator of high-quality practice. This claim echoes Dewey's emphasis on the important role that the teacher has, not in training children in a set of skills, but of shaping their thinking as well as their character through social interaction. Good teachers, Dewey argued, have intellectual curiosity and a passion for subjects, such as literacy, but are also invested in learning more about how children learn those subjects. Dewey promoted the educators' role in children's natural play, advocating playful methods as a way for teachers to foster experiential learning, voluntary participation and social order. Teachers should engage children in deep and complex reflective thought through questioning and problem solving which is not about 'thinking harder' but 'thinking differently' (1910, p.12).

Susan Isaacs (1885–1948)

Isaacs has expanded our understanding of the importance of play in children's learning by incorporating psychological theories of child development into Froebelian and Montessori approaches. She set up the Malting House School in Cambridge, England (1924–29) as an experiment in which to apply her scientific methods of observation and study children in a free play learning environment. Although the school only lasted for five years, Isaacs became a passionate promoter of nursery schooling, viewing it as an extension of what is learnt in the home; as an upbringing that offers social experience, and fosters positive relationships with adults and peers. Isaacs promoted cooperative play between children as a means to support this aspect of children's social development.

Isaacs also adopted certain features of psychoanalysis to frame her approach to play. She felt that children's play was a form of self-expression that provided them with opportunities to release their true feelings safely, and to rehearse different ways of dealing with their emotions. Children's tendencies and interests, both good and bad, demonstrated within their play needed to be acknowledged by others. In this way, Isaacs prioritised the child's voice in her work, rather than those of adults speaking for children (Bar-Haim, 2017).

Adults as teachers in Isaacs' nursery school were an important part of the learning environment providing children with the security and guidance needed to form successful bonds with others. Close observations to provide extensive records of children were needed for teachers to 'know' the children.

By providing opportunities for expression, free play could be understood as the vehicle for development. She wrote that play was the 'breath of life to the child, since it is through play activities that he finds mental ease, and can work upon his wishes, fears and fantasies so as to integrate them into a living personality' (Isaacs, 1951, p. 210). Together with the emotional benefits that play could support, Isaacs also saw it as a means for practical experimentation and discovery. Isaacs was hugely influential in popularising nursery provision through her ability to communicate with the public in many forms. She eventually became the Head of the Department of Child Development at the London Institute of Education.

Loris Malaguzzi (1920–1994)

Malaguzzi, a psychologist and school teacher, was instrumental in developing the influential Reggio Emilia approach to young children's education; an approach which is based on the principle that all children are capable, expressive and knowledgeable. Reggio Emilia is a town in North East Italy, and Malaguzzi's ideas about play and learning were born from the political context, and the ethical responses to this part of Italy after the Second World War. The Reggio Emilia movement was founded on principles directly opposed to the fascist ideas that had taken hold of Italy before and during the war. Instead, what Malaguzzi as a teacher proposed alongside other members of the community was an early childhood education based on progressive values, democracy and individuality. The child was viewed as having extraordinary potential for learning, able to construct their own experiences of the world. Key to this approach is a recognition of the child as subject to rights whose participation is essential for their development, but also for the cultural development of the community (Reggio Children, Reggio Emilia Approach, n.d.)

You can see traces of other play pioneers' ideas in Malaguzzi's theory of early education and play, particularly Dewey's focus on how children and teachers can create the curriculum together through shared experience. Malaguzzi was also influenced by theorists such as Vygotsky and Bruner who were interested in how children construct knowledge through their social and cultural interactions (these ideas will be discussed further in Chapter 2). His ideas evolved as he worked together with teachers, artists, parents and other staff within the Reggio Emilia's municipal infant-toddler centres and preschools. Through this collaboration, an understanding of a 'contextual' curriculum was created, one where everyone in the community, particularly children, can participate (Rinaldi, 2005).

Malaguzzi helps us understand his ideas about young children's literacy through his poem 'The One Hundred Languages of Children'. Read the poem found here: www.reggiochildren.it/en/reggio-emilia-approach/100-linguaggi-en/ and reflect on what Malaguzzi is saying about how young children are viewed by society and schools.

The poem outlines the multiple ways in which children can be creative in expressing their thoughts and feelings and how this capacity is ignored within traditional curriculum models. Malaguzzi argues that children's experience of the world is woven together through their use of different resources from which they are able to develop techniques and skills to represent their ideas. The Reggio Emilia approach extends our notion of the concept of language to languages (plural), moving ideas of expression and symbolism beyond the verbal and written form. Space is given to both verbal and non-verbal languages through sculpture, drawing, dance and dramatic play, as well as speech and writing.

Reggio preschools foreground the aesthetic space as an activator of learning so that children can develop an appreciation of beauty and design and be stimulated by the visual and poetic languages they encounter (Vecchi, 2010). This focus provides us with a deeper recognition of the importance of symbolising ideas using tools and materials, fundamental in supporting young children's literacies. The Reggio Emilia approach also encourages practitioners to develop environments that are listening spaces – a gesture of care towards the child and parent that values the diversity of experience and cultures of families and children (Dahlberg and Moss, 2005). This approach to listening is described by Rinaldi (2005, p. 65) as,

> sensitivity to the patterns that connect, to that which connects us to others, abandoning ourselves to the conviction that our understanding and our own being are but small parts of a broader, more integrated knowledge that holds the universe together.

Building this educator–parent–child dialogue is essential for sharing and constructing knowledge about, and with, the child. The child's languages are 'documented' by a Reggio Emilia practitioner and made visible to the whole Reggio Emilia Community. More explanation of how Reggio Emilia pedagogy supports young children's literacies can be found in Chapter 8.

The following case study highlights how observation and 'listening to children' provides the basis for Sheena's discussion with her colleagues. These reflections lead to a reorganisation of the provision in the setting and more creative outcomes for the children.

Case Study

Observing and Listening to Children

Sheena observes a small group of three children who are playing as usual in the construction area of the nursery. This is an area of the setting where they can independently access low level boxes of different types of construction toys such as blocks, bricks, cogs and small objects. After being introduced to Nicholson's (1971) theory of 'loose parts' play on a recent professional

(Continued)

development course (see Chapter 7), Sheena wants to enable better access to different materials and objects to facilitate the children's creative thinking. Sheena notes that today, the group are working cooperatively, building a castle. She has noticed that this is their daily activity of choice. Sheena also observes that while they work well together, they prevent other children from also using the area and accessing the boxes of construction toys because they spread their castle structures over the floor space in between the shelving. While Sheena continues to watch and listen, she notices that when other children are more persistent in accessing the construction resources, it causes conflict as they accidently knock over the castle structures in their desire to move the boxes away from the construction area to play with them in another area of the setting.

During a staff meeting, Sheena feels that this is important enough to discuss and shares her observations. Other staff respond that they have noticed the repetitive nature of the play of this group of three children. They too have also seen the challenges that this poses for other children's access to the play equipment. Sheena's observations lead to a discussion about the value of enabling children to be able to make their own decisions about what and who to play with. One of Sheena's colleagues remind the team that the Early Years Foundation Stage (EYFS, 2021) characteristics of effective learning promote the importance of children's ideas and choosing to do things independently. Staff agree and begin to discuss how the environment might be reorganised to enable children to access all of the available resources without potential conflict. By the end of the discussion, the team decide to involve the children in a reorganisation of the resources based on Sheena's observations.

The following day, Sheena leads the children in a discussion about the location of resources, explaining that she has noticed that sometimes children are finding it difficult to access resources. She asks what the children think could be done to enable them to get their toys out without treading on others' toys. Sheena notes that the children respond positively with ideas before deciding that they would like to be able to move the resources into other areas of the setting to play with. Decisions are reached to move the shelving and move some of the furniture.

Sheena's observations and responses to the learning environment will now enable all children to access the resources at any time and to take them to their desired area to play with. The children all agreed that they will return the toys to the correct storage areas once they have finished playing with them. In subsequent days, Sheena observes that the children have become more creative in their plan and that the small group who had been enjoying building castles have been building them outside on the grass where they are able to use sticks and stones to make drawbridges and redeploying the water containers to make moats.

Reflective questions

Why is it important for professionals/practitioners to observe children in their environments?

What do you think the benefits of enabling children to choose where to take the resources are?

Why do you think the children were included in decision making about the location of resources?

Do you think that this change appears effective? Why?

What are the implications for your own practice?

Different types/features of play

Play is repeatedly heralded as activity that supports children's psychological, socio-emotional and physical development. In order to examine how this happens it is often divided up (particularly in psychological studies) into different categories. These play types have distinct characteristics that help researchers to 'operationalise' complex play behaviours so that there is a shared understanding of what is being studied (Howard, 2018). Piaget (1951) identified three types of play echoing his theory about the stages of children's cognitive development: practice play, symbolic play and games with rules. Whitebread (2012) in his overview of published literature in the field identified five categories of play: physical play, play with objects, symbolic play, pretence/socio-dramatic play and games with rules. Wood and Attfield (2005) have also attempted to categorise a range of play activity, organising these into role play, imaginative play, socio-dramatic play, heuristic play, constructive play, fantasy play, free-flow play, structured play, rough and tumble play, 'all of which involve a wide range of activities and behaviours and result in varied learning and developmental outcomes' (p. 5).

Problems arise, however, by sorting play into different criteria in this way. For example, when children play, they move in and out of these different forms of play, often bringing different features of each play type together and blurring the distinctions. These fixed categories also assume a universality of children's experience, ignoring the fact that globally there are many versions of childhood shaped by social, cultural and material factors which affect how play 'looks' and how it is 'made up' dependent on the different spaces and places in which it takes place. The adult viewpoint is also foregrounded in sorting play in this way, without children's perspectives taken into consideration. Intriguingly, children categorise play very differently to adults; for example, they distinguish differences dependent on the space in which it occurs, and whether their peers are included (Howard, 2002, Howard et al., 2006). They also make clear distinctions between play and work, with levels of adult control a defining feature; for example, McInnes' (2019) research showed that children defined any activity with adults present as not being play at all.

As a Froebelian thinker, Tina Bruce (2011) advocates the importance of the child leading and managing her own play, sometimes known as free-flow play. To ascertain what play looks like – what it is as well as what it is not – she has identified 12 corresponding features that she argues are necessary aspects of free-flow play:

1. Children use first-hand experiences from life.
2. Children make up rules as they play in order to keep control.
3. Children symbolically represent as they play, making and adapting play props.
4. Children choose to play – they cannot be made to play.
5. Children rehearse their future in their role play.
6. Children sometimes play alone.
7. Children pretend when they play.
8. Children play with adults and other children cooperatively in pairs or groups.
9. Children have a personal play agenda, which may or may not be shared.
10. Children are deeply involved and difficult to distract from their deep learning as they wallow in their play and learning.
11. Children try out their most recently acquired skills and competences, as if celebrating what they know.
12. Children coordinate ideas and feelings and make sense of relationships with their families, friends and cultures.

Reflection

Are there any features of play listed above that you notice children in your setting experiencing more than others? Why do you think that is? Are there any other attributes of free-flow play that you think could be added to Tina Bruce's list?

Problematising play

One of the hardest day-to-day challenges practitioners and teachers have is how to employ play, particularly free-flow play, in an outcome-focused curriculum. Early years pedagogical practice, where play as learning is advocated, is commonly organised along a play–work continuum, with play positioned as 'freely chosen' and 'open-ended' at one end and 'non-play' (teacher-directed activity)

at the other (Wood and Attfield, 2005). The EYFS as a framework for organising pedagogical play embraces this continuum by stating that 'Children learn
by leading their own play, and by taking part in play which is guided by adults'.
However, the adult has a significant steer in this play provision as 'Practitioners
need to decide what they want children in their setting to learn, and the most
effective ways to teach it' (DfE, 2021, p. 16).

Judging the balance between child-led and educator-led play can have dramatic
effects on the play experiences of children and requires deep levels of reflection
about how to make sure any adult interaction in children's play has value (Fisher,
2016). Knowing when it is best to intervene and structure children's play activity
and when best to 'sit back' and let children lead, involves complex decision making which calls into question the stability of authority in the adult–child relationship. Smidt (2011, p. 2) alludes to this turbulence by posing the question 'where
is the role of the practitioner in play where the child is in control of the agenda?'
Moyles' (1989) play spiral model helps demonstrate how children's learning can
move in circular fashion between free play to directed play in recursive and incre-
mental movements, showing the importance of the role of the practitioner in
supporting and extending play. Nonetheless, the efficacy of this model lies with
the flexibility and intuitiveness of the practitioner. The organisation of play by
adults in any form, however knowledgeable, sensitive and supportive, carries
with it a fundamental problem by disrupting our philosophical understanding of
what play is – activity that is essentially powered by children's own interests and
intrinsic motivation (Else, 2009).

Reflection

Who do you think should lead play, the adult or the child? Why? Are your answers
different if the type of play changes?

It has also been argued that play is often manipulated to meet adult agendas
(Goouch, 2014). This manoeuvring is evident in the current discourse around play
pedagogy in England's reception classrooms developed as a consequence of the
data-driven school environment where the quality of practice is judged by how
well children achieve the Early Learning Goals. Reception teachers have attested
to the anxiety at leadership level in schools around play, with the word itself being
discouraged, and alternative descriptions such as 'discovery learning', which have
more learning intent, being used as alternatives (Smith, 2018). Ofsted's publication *Bold Beginnings* (2017), an examination of play from a school leadership perspective, has raised issues about how play is organised and its validity as a learning
tool in reception teaching. This is further underlined in the Education Endowment Foundation's production of the Early Years Toolkit which stresses the need

for play to be an 'effective' base for future measurable outcomes (EEF, 2017). *Bold Beginnings* has been heavily criticised by Early Childhood organisations such as TACTYC (2017) who are concerned about the policy implications of the tenuous claims made in these publications which ignore the value of play for child development and question its role in learning, ignoring a wealth of contrary evidence.

The reason that play needs to prove its worth as 'effective' to children's long-term learning outcomes is a product of what Wood (2010) describes as the 'progress agenda'. The outcome of this agenda, particularly within the context of high stakes school accountability, is that children's play becomes controlled and monitored by powerful adults. But examine this closely and you will see that it is based on a particular assumption: that the value of play – its main function – is predominantly to support children's learning and development. As a consequence of this, how effectively play is utilised will have an impact on children's future-selves, and is therefore open to engineering.

This developmental approach to play, or 'eduplay', that validates play as educational advancement, has been advocated by Western play theorists throughout the centuries, but ignores some of the realities of children's play as subversive activity. As Sutton-Smith (1997) stressed, play may help children progress but it isn't necessarily about learning something beneficial; children can be unkind to others and be subjected to physical harm in their play, they can be destructive of materials and the environment, and seek out dangerous risks. Children's play can mirror power inequalities in society as they reinforce gender stereotypes in their role play. They can also become fixated and compulsive in their use of play objects. Evidence then that play isn't always about positive advancement, or constructive learning. Within an eduplay environment, these destabilising features of play will need to be regulated through policy and governed in practice to encourage play that is developmentally appropriate.

Reflection

Do you agree that play needs to be policed and governed in an educational environment to ensure that children are not able to engage in subversive play or do you think that they need to be able to engage in this to learn holistically about the world? What are the implications of this for your practice?

Western developmentalism is also founded on the premise that all children can and will play to learn naturally; however, children need to be encultured into play, with some children who haven't had experience of Western ideas of play put at a disadvantage when they are expected to play to learn (Brooker, 2002). Cannella and Viruru (2004) argue that play as development is culturally constructed by a dominant Western culture, one that views education as a means for social control, accountability and management by technicians. This reinforces inequalities and disadvantage, by discounting alternative versions of play. Instead, we need to look closely at how the social, cultural as well as material context in children's play is constructed (Burman, 2008). This deconstructing of play by critiquing the prevalent developmentalism that surrounds it, and how it is culturally performed, has led to more fundamental shifts in understanding the meaning of play.

Post-developmental and posthumanist theories of play

Moving beyond developmental frameworks and contesting these universal conceptions of play has resulted in the emergence of 'post-developmental' theories. Post-developmentalism rejects universal or standard experiences of play that children can be organised around; a rationalist view of play, where play experience can be measured and accounted for. Instead, play is viewed as expansive, organic and non-linear; a series of unique 'moment-to-moment' encounters. To understand play fully, therefore, is to recognise its diversity, rather than its linear trajectory with a single purpose. Braidotti (2017, p. 21) describes this human experience as 'we-are-in-this-together-but-we-are-not-one-and-the-same'. Children play not as unitary subjects, but as complex and multi-layered beings.

These theories reject fixed binary notions of play, e.g. adult–child, child–object, individual–social, virtual–non-virtual, as they are interested in how these aspects of play come together, their mutuality, and how relationships between them are formed as they merge together and as well as transgress (Lenz-Taguchi, 2010). To know more about play then we need to map the movements and relationships between different elements of children's play and how they are generated as an ensemble or 'assemblage' (Deleuze and Guattari, 2004). This places children back in the driving seat of play as they are the generators, with responsibilities for their play, and have power in how they perform it (Sellers, 2013). It also emphasises that learning language and literacy is less about learning vocabulary and grammar (our traditional focus) and more about encouraging children's participation in multisensory, connective events that bring together bodies, minds and the material world (Hackett, MacLure and McMahon, 2020).

This decentralisation has re-emphasised the place of children's bodies as the lived experience, rather than children's minds, as being at the centre of play; often described as embodiment, or the embodied experience. Even though this is an essential feature in many play pioneers' writings about play, it has been ignored in recent discussions that foregrounded children's thinking (Tobin, 2004). Re-focusing on the playing child as embodied, demonstrates how play has cultural significance; for example, Burke and Duncan's (2015) comparison of young children in early childhood education in New Zealand and Japan has uncovered how children's bodies are organised dependent on cultural expectations – this extends to what children wear, how noise is tolerated, as well as touch.

Karen Barad's work as a molecular physicist has also been influential in how we view the embodied child, where bodies, materials, culture, power and space come together within play. Barad (2007) suggests that our interests should not lie in either the human or the nonhuman, but the entanglements between the two. She states, 'We don't obtain knowledge by standing outside the world; we know because we are of the world' (cited in Jackson and Mazzei, 2013, p. 117). Importantly, Barad argues that materials have agency; that their molecular components affect the way that a child 'intra-acts' with it (2007, p. 33). This is important as it recognises that materials and geographical spaces are integral to how play is shaped. This happens as the child and the materials – both natural (water, sand, soil, and elements) as well as manufactured (carpet, plastic toys, book) – come together as intra-action. Conceptualising play as intra-active means focusing on children as 'players becoming capable of knowing in a variety of social and material relations comprising play(ful) encounters' (Rautio and Winston, 2015, p. 15). If you look again at the vignette at the beginning of the chapter you will see how Ben and Lucy's bodies, the sand and the stick they are playing with can be viewed in this way as they are intra-acting with the material world that they are within.

Reflection

Can you remember the materials or resources that you played with as a child? Or the particular spaces in which you enjoyed playing? How did these materials and spaces affect how you played?

These contemporary ideas of young children's play do not try to define what play is, rather they attempt to understand the complexity of its construction. This helps us to create a deeper understanding of the philosophies that the pioneers of play – Froebel, Montessori, Dewey, Isaacs and Malaguzzi – advocated, and provide alternative forums in which we can 'play with' their ideas to help us appreciate how play provides rich opportunities for multilple literacies.

Practice ideas

The following ideas are based on what we have learned about play from our educational experience with young children. We hope that they will inspire you to develop excellent play practices with children:

- Get creative! Old plastic milk containers can be filled with sand or water and used to build walls. If you collect clean large and small containers, such as boxes, plastic crates, tyres, tubes and drinks bottles that are surplus to requirements, you can use these to make structures.
- Giant chalk is a great resource for the outdoors. (You can wash it away when you have finished.) Encourage children to draw a road or a path and accompanying signs to travel on with their bikes, trikes and scooters.
- Plant a herb garden. You don't even need a garden for this. You can use pots if you like. Children love to dig and plant. Watching the plants grow and nurturing them teaches children about being careful and patient and they will be rewarded with a sensory experience as they pick the herbs. You could even use these to cook with too!
- Tents are not just for the outdoors! Create a cosy reading nook that entices children to curl up with a good book inside. Fill a small tent with cushions and an array of picture books and soft toys.
- Place small world people, cars, animals, houses, etc. next to shallow boxes of damp sand. Children can recreate their favourite stories and scenarios and mould the sand into different environments.

In summary

- Play pioneers from the past show us that young children's play is essential for their learning and oneness with the world.
- As children play they connect to their material world and each other in order to express who they are and represent their experience.
- Educators need to listen and observe children's play carefully so that they can follow children's lead in improving play opportunities without undermining it.
- Posthuman theorists reject developmental views of play and instead recognise it as a complex and unpredictable entanglement of human and non-human elements.

Having read this chapter, here are some **discussion questions** to help you in planning for young children's play in the future:

1. What play pioneers' ideas would you advocate in supporting children's play activity?

2. Do you have a 'philosophy' of play, i.e. your own theory about what play is, what it means, and how it should be organised?

Further recommended reading

Brooker, L. and Edwards, S. (Eds.) (2010) *Engaging Play*. Maidenhead, Berkshire: Open University Press.

The chapters in this edited book are written by a range of international researchers. It will help you to examine some of the current tensions that exist in understanding what play is for, how it is being reconceptualised, and how professionals are re-thinking how play can be organised for young children.

Moyles, J. (Ed.) (2014) *The Excellence of Play* (4th ed.). Maidenhead, Berkshire: Open University Press.

Written by many key experts in the field of early education, this book provides a thorough examination of the key issues and arguments that surround pedagogies of play. It is highly recommended as a way to build your understanding of the content presented in this chapter.

2

PLAYFUL ENCOUNTERS: LANGUAGE AND MULTIMODAL COMMUNICATION

This chapter will

- introduce you to Vygotsky, Chomsky and Bruner's theories of language development;
- build your understanding of the important role that adults have in supporting children's communication and language;
- help you to identify multimodal communication within children's play;
- provide you with an understanding of how and why babies communicate and how to support them to do so.

As soon as we are born, we have a desire to show what we think, feel and need to others. Human babies want to communicate or 'tell' something about themselves that others can understand. Language as speech and gesture as well as other ways of communicative movements help young children to construct personal stories to share with others; play is a conduit for this, enabling children to create stories about the things that are important to them. Within play, children are able to select from a range of modes how to symbolise as closely as they can, what they are thinking, feeling and experiencing; it could be through gesture, dance, speech, drawing, touch, song, writing, and so forth, just as Malaguzzi described in his 'The One Hundred Languages of Children' poem (see Chapter 1).

This chapter will introduce you to major theories of language development and communication. We will look at how closely language is linked to thinking and knowledge, and show that language isn't just a means for knowing something, but also a way of expressing what we know to others, this being the catalyst for its production. We will also explore how language is expressed and symbolised in multiple ways within play for different purposes, not only as cognition (a thinking process), but also a way of exploring the social and emotional world with bodies and materials. Towards the end of the chapter we will look in more detail at how playful communication begins and the mutual responsiveness between carers and babies that is necessary for children to learn and use language and other forms of communication with others. As you read through this chapter consider the connections that exist between the theories of language and the philosophies of play outlined in Chapter 1.

. To help you understand how play functions as a necessary feature of very young children's language and communication, read the vignette that follows. Think about how Mattias' father is 'playing' with his son, taking turns in conversation, matching the pitch and tone of his responses to 'tune into' Mattias' speech. There are pauses while Mattias is expected to respond as a necessary part of the conversation. Within this affectionate episode, Mattias is learning that as a person he is responded to and is expected to respond in return.

Vignette

Letting babies lead playful conversation

Four-month-old Baby Mattias is sitting on his mother's knee next to his father who is gently calling his name. He bobs his head sideways to focus his gaze on his dad who says to him 'what are you doing?'. Mattias bobs his head back towards the direction that his mother is facing. His dad calls his name again and when Mattias responds by turning his head towards him once more, Dad pokes out his tongue. This catches Mattias' attention and captured by this action he opens and closes his mouth in response. His dad gently blows air on his face and Mattias responds by moving his head backwards and closing his eyes. When he opens them again, Dad repeats this action, laughing. Mattias gurgles with pleasure in response which leads his father to ask in a high-pitched sing song voice, 'what are you saying?'. Mattias repeats his gurgle and his father replies 'are you laughing?' before tickling his tummy.

When Mattias and his father are interacting, they are both learning from each other about what language is and they are doing this as part of the 'learning culture' (the ways of being and behaving together) within their family. The theories below explain in detail how Mattias is able to learn language in this way.

Theoretical perspectives on language as human development

Vygotsky

Lev Vygotsky's work has been hugely influential in framing our understanding of the social and cultural construction of language learning. Vygotsky was interested in the movement of development within the child, from the external social experience to the internal psychological construction of their learning. In the vignette above for example, you can see how Mattias is responding to the social experience he is sharing with his father – this social experience will be shaping his internal thinking. Vygotsky carried out a series of experiments with children to demonstrate how this process of internalisation and development occurred. His most famous work written in 1934 and translated from Russian in the 1980s is often published with the title *Thought and Language* (1986), but as Vygotsky emphasised the importance of language as an action it is more accurately titled *Thinking and Speaking*. It provides us with a detailed examination of how a child's ideas and knowledge are formed as a process of thinking within the social world where speech and words are carriers of meaning. Vygotsky explained that 'a thought is born through words. A word devoid of thought is a dead thing… an empty sound' (p. 212) and that 'thought development is determined by language' (p. 94).

For Vygotsky, thinking and language cannot occur in a vacuum; it needs tools and signs for it to take shape. Linguistic tools such as gesture or gaze in very young or non-verbal children, as well as speech, carry meanings associated with how they are used within particular sociocultural environments. Vygotsky proposed that through speech, thought finds 'expression' and this expression is understood within the social context. This happens when the development of our 'inner speech', a cognitively invisible process, comes into being from the appropriation of the social speech we experience. His argument stresses that communicative practices are culturally and socially mediated, i.e. they are socially constructed. What is noteworthy here is Vygotsky's emphasis on the centrality of social relationships in the first steps of learning, recognising that children's cognitive development is culturally saturated (Mercer, 1994, p. 93). The cultural environment of the child, therefore, drives their unique development; an idea that has been taken up and extended by many subsequent researchers exploring children's development of language. In the vignette, Mattias' father pokes out his tongue to invoke a reaction to his affectionate humour. He is helping Mattias to recognise and learn with the cultural resources he is familiar with.

In Vygotsky's (1986) theory there are three types or forms of language that emerge as children develop. First, social speech which is the external communication that children typically develop from the age of two to help them communicate or speak, with others. Second, private or egocentric speech developing after the age of three, which is a self-directed form helping children to think and construct their ideas as a 'self-dialogue'. Finally, from about the age of seven, these prior forms of speech transform into inner speech which arises as an internal dialogue, a silent language which functions to self-regulate our thinking and behaviour. Inner speech is a way for children to plan what they want to do and be reflective. Important factors in learning to read and write.

You can see here that Vygotsky saw language is an accelerator for understanding the world and ourselves. An essential part of this is the important role that adults have in supporting children's construction of thought. He explains how adults, or a more knowledgeable other (MKO) such as a more experienced child, assists a child's learning by identifying what a child is able to do alone, and what they can do with support. With careful assessment, a teacher, practitioner or parent is able to identify the gap between these two. Vygotsky called this gap the Zone of Proximal Development (ZPD). Adults and MKOs function to shape a child's development within their play as they guide the child's participation, providing support, direction, challenge. This is described by Rogoff (1990) as an apprenticeship in thinking. In play experiences, as seen in Chapter 1, the term sustained shared thinking (SST) is used to define this process of scaffolding a child's thinking. Siraj-Blatchford (2009, p. 79) describes SST as,

> an effective pedagogic interaction, where two or more individuals work together in an intellectual way to solve a problem, clarify a concept, evaluate activities, or extend a narrative.

Reflection

How was Mattias' father supporting his son's thinking? How was he encouraging him to engage in embodied interactions and social speech?

For Vygotsky, play experiences, particularly imaginative play, provide children with an impetus for development. In his work, 'Play and Its Role in the Mental Development of the Child' (1967) he argued that children's imaginative play isn't merely exploration, without an aim or purpose, but is activity that extends thinking about people, materials and objects (Smidt, 2011). Play, therefore, is a transitionary stage towards higher reasoning. He wrote that,

> Action in the imaginative sphere, in an imaginary situation, the creation of voluntary intentions, and the formation of real-life plans and volitional motives — all appear in play and make it the highest level of preschool development. (Vygotsky, 1967, p. 16)

Vygotsky supported make-believe play, rather than sensory play. He saw the importance of children using objects imaginatively as a way of helping them to extend their thinking beyond their own concrete (actual and real) experiences. For example, a child may cuddle a bundle of tea towels usually used to dry dishes and imagine that they are a new baby brother or hold a toy brick to their ear and make-believe it is a mobile phone. Imaginative play helps children to understand that one object can represent another and that things can symbolise other things. By having the opportunity to play in this way, children will be able to understand that just as an object can potentially become something else, the marks that form the shape of a letter can come to symbolise a sound. Playful imagination is therefore an incredibly important aspect of reading and writing, as we need to be able to suspend our belief that text making isn't just squiggles or marks on paper or screen, but is an 'object' or alternatively a 'form' that has the potential to represent our ideas and those of others.

As children play, the child's intentionality as a player, what their aims and objectives are, is important, as their personal purpose in playing, either alone or with others, helps them to regulate and control the learning activity they are engaged in (Bodrova and Leong, 2015). Vygotsky argued that imaginative play, as a way of supporting the individual management of language and thought, needs to be led by the child and supported by the adult or MKO. We will find out more about how adults can increase opportunities for language and literacy through imaginative play in Chapter 3.

Chomsky

Noam Chomsky (1965, 1986) offers us an alternative perspective on language development by stressing its innate biological features. His theory focuses on a child's in-built 'machinery', the internal cognitive systems of thought that are 'native' to the child. This idea doesn't negate all the social and cultural (environmental) factors highlighted by Vygotsky, but does raise some interesting questions about what is powering the development of language and how our language is structured. It also positions the child not as a blank slate, but as having natural competencies and potential. Chomsky's theory was developed as a rejection of dominant behaviourist ideas that propose that children learn language through positive reinforcement of what they hear and see. He argued that this didn't explain how children know complex language structures that they haven't heard before, or why it is that children universally appear to go through similar processes in acquiring the use of language.

Chomsky's theoretical explanation of how children learn language is that every child has an internal language device innate to them – the Language Acquisition Device (LAD), which provides them with the ability to organise language in a grammatical form so that it makes logical sense. This is the theory of Universal Grammar, where the child is born with all of the grammatical information about nouns, verbs, syntax, etc. that they need once they are exposed to vocabulary to be able to create their own sentences. Chomsky demonstrated this by stressing a poverty of the stimulus, where the linguistic input that children experience, what they have heard and already tried out by speaking to others, is not sufficient to explain how they are able to 'know' about how language is structured. To illustrate this, when young children speak they sometimes make grammatical mistakes by misapplying or over-compensating grammatical rules, for example they may say 'I wented', rather than 'I went', or state 'my drawing is betterer', rather than 'my drawing is better'. The child will not have heard an adult saying 'wented' or 'betterer', proving that they are generating these grammatical patterns internally and independently, not through copying others or by having others co-construct these sentences with them as Vygotsky would argue. Instead, they are hypothesising using the inherent grammatical knowledge they have (Pinker, 1994), therefore, all children need from their environment are the words of their given language to feed into their internal system. The environment that the child is born into will give energy to the child's internal device, but it is the innate processing machinery that shapes it into meaningful structures.

Reflection

As adults we often find young children's over-compensation of grammatical rules a delight. Can you think of any examples that you have overheard young children say that may prove Chomsky's theory?

In recent years, Chomsky's assumptions about Universal Grammar have been challenged by studies that show that languages differ from each other in profound ways, with very few true universal elements between them (Evans, 2014). This diversity of language – these different grammars and their social and cultural variance – is overlooked in Chomsky's work. The essential nativist approach that Chomsky takes has also been criticised as it foregrounds children's genetic or natural endowment for language and downplays the cultural differences that exist in how language is used by people. Language can't merely be viewed as a universal grammatical operation when we can see that cultural environment affects how it is formed and how it functions. For example, different languages use sounds, tones and rhythms differently to convey social and cultural meanings, and this can only be learnt through social interaction.

Bruner

Jerome Bruner's work reinforces the importance of the social environment, and particularly the interactional element of language learning. Like Chomsky, he claims that children are born with the internal mechanisms to learn language; however, he argues that the cultural environment is an essential ingredient. Bruner emphasises the importance of the external experience that surrounds the child, or the Language Acquisition Support System, a network of people and resources that scaffold and support the child's language to develop. Adopted from Vygotskian theory, he identifies scaffolding as,

> the steps taken to reduce the degrees of freedom in carrying out some task so that the child can concentrate on the difficult skill she is in the process of acquiring. (Bruner, 1978, p. 19)

Bruner stresses the importance of shared everyday language routines and repetition that enables the child, through practice and habits, to map the linguistic codes that they need to be able to use grammar and develop vocabulary. This process needs facilitation by others; these systems of scaffolding are external and operate through shared joint action and attention. Hence, Bruner like John Dewey (see Chapter 1), was a supporter of active learning, focusing on the child's social learning experience. And like Vygotsky, Bruner realised that play was an important facilitator for language, particularly when children and adults played together as this gave them the ability to share ideas about real and imaginary worlds. He visited the Reggio Emilia preschools (discussed in Chapter 8) and was inspired by their learning environment where he felt that the use of the mind, imagination and materials came together to unlock the code of language and meaning making (Bruner, 1986). Extending these ideas further, his most recent work focused on the role that narrative has in helping children construct an understanding of their lives and those of others. He argued that narrative is central to how we structure our thoughts and how we invent stories about who we are and the world we live in (Bruner, 1992). Narratives tread the line between what is actual or real, and what is imagined, and play is a vehicle for facilitating this process.

The following case study highlights the important role that adults have in reciprocating play-based encounters and helping to extend children's play narratives, when invited to do so.

Case Study

Finding Asha's Voice

Four-year-old Asha has happily settled into her Reception class. It has been observed by her teacher, Tom, that she is keen to play with others, engaging her friends through gesture, the direction of her gaze and the movement of her body. However, she rarely speaks to other adults or children either inside or outside of the classroom setting. Her grandmother (who is her main carer) has said that she talks non-stop at home which allays any concerns about hearing or speech. While being conscious that Asha is communicating through 'body language', Tom begins to ask himself how he could support and scaffold Asha

(Continued)

to speak to others. He recognises the importance of words in understanding how Asha is making meaning in her play and representing her thoughts verbally for others to respond to (Vygotsky, 1978). Tom also understands the importance of social and emotional wellbeing in supporting learning (EYFS, DfE, 2021).

Tom decides that as Asha is now happily settled, he should sensitively play near to Asha during child-initiated play so that he can gently encourage her to speak aloud. Tom takes care not to take over her play by playing in parallel and works on building her trust gradually. Tom 'talks aloud' about what he is doing as a way of modelling his thinking aloud for Asha to hear. He notices that she is responding to this through eye contact and smiling which encourages him to continue with this strategy. After a while, he notices that Asha is responding physically by handing him objects so that he can continue with his play. He reciprocates by handing the objects back once he has 'used' them. Tom intends to continue with speaking his play narratives aloud for a bit longer as a way of modelling his thinking through language (Bruner, 1992) for Asha to respond to. He realises that he needs to be patient while she builds her confidence in speaking aloud. After a week or so of using this strategy, Tom celebrates quietly to himself as Asha asks him one morning if he wants to make an animal park with her.

Reflective questions

Adopting ideas from either Vygotsky, Chomsky or Bruner, how would you have supported Asha to 'find her voice' in the reception classroom? Would you do anything differently to Tom?

What questions would you ask her grandmother to find out more about her language use at home?

What activities could you plan to encourage Asha to speak more readily to other children?

Narrative is central to how we structure our thoughts and how we invent stories about who we are and the world we live in with others (Bruner, 1992). Narratives tread the line between what is actual or real, and what is imagined, and play is a vehicle for facilitating this process. By building on Vygotsky's ideas about how children use objects imaginatively in their play, Bruner was able to identify more clearly how language provides us with a means of representation. This is incredibly important in understanding how literacies work. Literacy has important elements of representation that function to show others what you know. To encourage young children's literacies, we want them to be able to represent their ideas, feelings, experiences in as many different ways as possible. Bruner identified three ways in which children's knowledge about the world are represented, or modes of representation (Bruner, 1966). Bruner's three modes of representation are enactive, iconic and symbolic. These shouldn't be viewed as stages of development, rather as loosely organised junctures where children's thinking, and therefore their ability to represent ideas, get transformed.

Enactive representation

This is based on the actions of the child. It is prevalent in the first year of life and is a completely embodied, physical mode where the child's ability to show what they can do is rooted purely on the physical memory of doing things. This doesn't leave us as we get older; as adults we often refer to 'muscle memory' when we are able to do something physically, and we appear to 'know' how to ride a bike or drive a car without thinking. Bruner agrees that this isn't actually thinking as we can't really describe what we are doing to ourselves or others; we have limited ability to represent it, we just know from doing it, the action itself being the representation.

Iconic representation

Associated with children from one to six years old, this mode involves children being able to internally 'picture' the idea in their mind. It is closely linked to imagination and moves thinking into different realms where we are able to visualise doing something, and then be able to tell others about it, through for example, gesture, speech, touch or movement. This image-based mode is a very 'freeing' event for children and is a really important transition to the next stage.

Symbolic representation

This is where language moves towards culturally recognised literacies. In this mode, a child's knowledge of the world is translated into symbols and codes which can be manipulated in multiple ways. As examples of these symbols or codes think of drawings, written text or musical notation. As the child plays with these symbols and works out the codes associated with them, they are able to represent their thinking of others, and then in turn the 'reader' of their symbols can understand what the child means. Children also use these symbols to enhance and expand their thinking by interacting with how others symbolised their actions and thinking. To understand how this works, consider how you are reading this now; you are looking at the symbols that represent the writers' ideas, as well as making sense of them through your own experience – so reading is active, responsive and extends thinking, but we can say the same when children are drawing together, or connecting through many other modes of literacy.

Playing or interacting with representative symbols in this way is a very creative thinking process which is enhanced by practice and experience.

It is very important then that young children are given time and resources to develop these different representational modes as they move towards more formalised literacy. As you will see in the coming chapters, without these experiences children will not know the full potential that different literacies have to transform their ideas.

Multimodal communication

The modes that Bruner introduced us to are invaluable in understanding children's language development; however, current researchers are increasingly interested in the ways that children make meaning of their world beyond traditional ideas of language that are focused on speech. The argument being that language as thinking with spoken words and text does not provide us with a full enough explanation of the many channels of representation or modes of communication that children have at their disposal, particularly in the current digital age (Kress and Van Leeuwen, 2001). Instead, researchers are focusing on diverse forms of communication – as multiple modes – that children use to express their ideas. These multimodal approaches are able to expand our understanding of young children's communication by examining how humans symbolise their ideas through diverse visual, aural, embodied and spatial elements (MODE, 2012). They support a more inclusive understanding of young children's communication abilities, as while they recognise the structures of language within some modes, they also consider how other modes of communication, ones that cannot be 'known' in terms of language description combine to create an ensemble of meaning for children. Therefore, a child who is non-verbal will be using many different ways of communicating and representing their ideas by using other modes that are equally as important as speech.

The multimodal approach to literacy is based on the theory of social semiotics. Semiotics is the study of signs and symbols and how they are used in social life (Saussure, 1966). Social semiotics focuses on how social structures and processes form these signs and create signification (meaning) (Halliday, 1978). Recognising this theory, we can see that children's sign making is a socially functional literate activity (Jewitt, 2011, p. 30), so it is important to listen to and observe how all of these signs are created. Taking a multimodal approach helps us to do this. To listen and hear a child properly, what they may be expressing or signifying to others, we need to observe carefully how children play with the different modes of communication they have at their disposal. We need to view this as a process of collective meaning making, as children are bringing different modes together as an ensemble within their play (Mavers, 2011). As we will see in the next section about conversations with babies, identifying how these different modes of expression come together deepens our understanding of how even our youngest children are able to communicate in varied and complex ways.

Importantly, in multimodal approaches all modes of representation and communication have potentialities and constraints, or 'modal affordances' (Kress, 2010, p. 82). These are culturally assigned by their usage and determine what it is possible to 'say' with them, and also what can't be 'said'. As an example, children will use touch as a form of communication differently dependent on the contexts and people involved as these environments will afford different meanings to touch; for instance it may be used differently with friends in the park than it is with close family members at home. Therefore, all modes of communication are shaped by their cultural environment; they are afforded different uses dependent on the context. When, we are working with children to support their language and communication, we need to be aware of how different modes of communication can be limited by how we frame their usage.

Examples of how researchers have used these approaches include Rosie Flewitt's multimodal video case studies of children in home and preschools (2005, 2006). The analysis she makes of how children interact using different modes of communication (talk, gesture, movement, gaze, and so on) demonstrates the multifunctional use of different modalities by children as socially organised, intentional meaning making. Flewitt's work helps us to recognise the range of communication that children use to construct meaning together, how these are shaped by their day-to-day use within the learning space, providing us with a broader understanding of language and how to observe it, particularly within early years environments.

Taking a multimodal approach overlaps to a certain extent with posthumanist ideas as discussed in Chapter 1, where space, time, materials, movement and bodies are all understood as important ways of playing. We will revisit these multimodal approaches in the proceeding chapters that look at different literacies to deepen your understanding of the importance of encouraging young children to play with diverse modes of communication.

In the case study that follows, consider how the adult helpers are being supported by the nursery manager to develop children's communication and language in a range of ways.

Case Study

Developing Children's Communication Through Action Songs

Jasmine, a nursery manager, has arranged for the children to visit a local farm. She has taken care to select a farm that is used to small children visiting and has facilities that enable the children to regularly clean and wash their hands so that they are able to see, hear and touch the animals. Jasmine plans to use this experience to extend the children's communication and

(Continued)

language. The day before the visit, Jasmine holds a meeting for the adults who will be supporting the children on the outing to share her intentions for the visit so that the children are well supported.

Jasmine ensures that the adults are all introduced to each other so that they can work effectively with each other during the trip. She has several volunteers who are relatives of the children to support the nursery practitioners. Jasmine explains that she wants to promote language and communication as much as possible by encouraging the children to make animal noises, sing songs and do actions. She asks the group to think of some ideas for songs and suggests that they have a go at practising these which results in lots of laughter as they have a go at the actions together in advance of the trip. The adults voice their appreciation as some were not able to recall all the words of the songs and others did not know some of the songs, so rehearsing these was a valuable learning experience for them.

Reflective questions

What assumptions might we make as educators about the knowledge that other adults hold?

How could the adults support the children to communicate what they were experiencing during the trip?

How else could the adults scaffold children's diverse modes of communication so that they can represent their trip to the farm through their play after the trip?

Our earliest conversations

Even before a child is born, they are busy interacting with their mother through the movements, touch and sound they share, and it is their mother (their face and touch) that they direct their attention too when they enter the world. Babies are wired to expect (and demand) social, emotional and creative interaction with others, and are seeking faces to not only imitate but to rhythmically respond to.

> Far from being passive recipients, responding only reflexively to stimuli – as was once thought – babies come into the world actively ready to communicate their needs, feelings and motives to other persons, as well as ready for sympathetic engagement of vocal, facial and gestural expression. (Dissanayake, 2000, p. 44)

Infants are capable from birth of mirroring or imitating the social actions of their carers. Lepage and Théoret (2007) have argued that there is a Mirror

Neuron System (MNS) in humans that is already present at birth and through experience is continually developed into adult life. Babies relate to and understand those around them by simulating within their own neural networks the pattern of activity that is evoked as they observe, act and share emotions and thoughts with others. We can deduce, therefore, that when new born babies are communicated with, this is stimulating systems of neural networks supporting them in developing their abilities to take part in further social acts.

The first year of life involves a huge amount of change for children in their understanding and use of language. During this time babies are making subjective sense of their native language by attentively listening to the patterns, intonations and sounds (phonemes) that they are witness to from the interactions around them. They will also be responding to what they hear by verbalising, making eye-contact and moving, and typically between six and eight months, their canonical babbling (e.g. bababa, dadada) emerges. This process, illustrated in our vignette at the beginning of the chapter, is dependent on reciprocity, meaning that it involves a mutually beneficial exchange between the carer and the baby, and is fundamentally a relational process.

These multimodal communicative encounters with babies can be viewed as playful events in that they involve joy, a sense of humour, and physical, social and cognitive spontaneity; all features of playfulness according to Lieberman (1977). They are also deeply emotional as a form of basic loving connection and a means for babies to develop empathy and a sense of who they are in the world – who and where they belong. Knowing this, we can argue that these early relational communicative encounters are vital not only for language, but also social and emotional development. It is worth noting that as children's language is being refined, their ability to communicate extended and their authorship expanded, an emotional dimension will always be an integral part. It is really important, therefore, that the carer is responsive to what the child is 'telling' them, and that they tune into the babies' needs and desires. Colwyn Trevarthen (2005) cites Daniel Stern (1993, 1999) in describing this practice as 'attunement'.

Trevarthen, a biologist with an interest in neuro-physiology, has helped us enormously to understand what is happening when babies express movement towards others as they learn about communication. He described this process as 'intersubjectivity'. Put simply, a sharing of minds (Smidt, 2018), where the child and carer are aware of each other and change their gestures, sounds and so on to accommodate each for the purpose of a shared intention. This can be viewed as a respectful and loving dialogue, a very early conversation, or protoconversation. Trevarthen (1999) describes in the quote below the sensitive dynamics of a new mother's intuitive readiness to share a protoconversation with her child.

> A mother greets her newborn in ecstatic cries with falling pitch, and by
> gentle fondling. She is unable to keep her eyes from the baby's face. She

touches hands, face, body with rhythmic care, and holds the infant close to her so they can join attention and greet one another. Her speech is a kind of singing, with high gliding gestures of pitch and repetition of regular gentle phrases on a graceful beat, leaving places for the infant to join in with coos, smiles and gestures of the hands or whole body. Every move of the baby elicits reaction from her. These exchanges are intricately coordinated with a subdued choreography that brings out matching rhythms and phrasing in mother and infant. (p. 174)

Reflection

Consider the vignette presented at the beginning of the chapter having read about Trevarthen's ideas. Do you think the vignette describes a protoconversation? What makes you think this?

Trevarthen also recognised that children will be experiencing this choreography in different social and cultural contexts. So how a baby is held, where they are positioned, how they are interacted with and by whom is dependent on external factors that will frame the intimate baby–carer communication. We also know from BabyLab observations (University of York, n.d.) that although the speech register is thought to be nearly universal, the style of speech used with babies varies from one culture to another and also between families within a single culture. Very young children may encounter similar cultural experiences of early language and communication, but these experiences may vary enormously and therefore it is important that teachers and practitioners find out about children's earliest experiences of language to understand the guidance and participation they have had.

Reflection

How might teachers and practitioners sensitively explore children's earliest experiences of language?

Communicative musicality

Trevarthen alongside his colleague Stephen Malloch also coined the term communicative musicality as a way of describing the sounds or melody between babies and their carers (Malloch and Trevarthen, 2009). For young infants, melodious speech and singing may not be distinct from each other but appear as 'sound play' and is received or heard in the same way that music is (Brandt et al., 2012). Infant Directed Speech (IDS), sometimes known as 'motherese' or 'parentese', is universally used by carers to communicate with babies and has distinctive musical features. Importantly, it does not lose the essential properties of speech, rather it supports these features. Not only does IDS exaggerate the aspects of conventional speech, it also incorporates some musical features such as sustained vowels and phrase-final lengthening, exaggerating others such as pitch range expansion (Fernald et al., 1989).

Positive emotional engagement is evident when carers sing with babies. In general, mothers smile more when they sing than when they speak (Trehub et al., 2015) and singing and musical speech generally contain happy vocalisations. The 'happy voice' qualities of singing and musical speech play an important role in regulating infant attention and appear more effective than other vocal modes (Corbeil et al., 2013).

Emotional elements are evident within the expression of music, for example loud and soft, crescendo and staccato, and these correspond with the physiological changes we experience through emotion. A significant aspect of singing is the emotional connection that can be made to others as music and singing is made together (Dissanayke, 2000). Infant-directed singing is often used to decrease distress and develop positive sensations. For example, when carers engaged in infant-directed singing, babies took almost nine minutes to get distressed (grimacing, crying and restlessness), roughly twice as long as when listening to infant-directed speech (Corbeil et al., 2016). There is also evidence that for babies the predictability of music in its temporal and pitch structure, generates expectations and then fulfilment as the song unfolds (Corbeil et al., 2013). Singing with children is therefore a really beneficial way to promote togetherness as well as an awareness of rhyme, rhythm and sound, important foundations for reading and writing.

Singing provides a way of affecting babies' emotional regulation and reducing the high arousal levels of distressed infants. It can be argued that singing with a baby should be considered a 'care moment', in which the carer is tuned into the emotional and physical needs of the baby and closeness is sought. Mualem and Klein (2013) in their study on the differences between play and musical interactions between mothers and one-year-old infants showed that the duration of physical contact and eye contact between mothers and their children were longer in the musical interactions than in the play interactions. When the mothers sang to their children, they tended to position them physically close to their own body. This physical closeness is also evident in Trehub et al.'s (2015) research where there is a clear link between mothers' use of rhythmic singing with their rhythmic head and arm movements that captures the babies' attention and distracts them from stress. It appears that infants are sensitive not only to rhythmic patterns but also to patterns of physical movement when they are moved by others as they are sung to.

Practice ideas

The following ideas may be useful in supporting children's language and communication:

- Sing nursery rhymes with children. (Don't worry about singing in tune. Children don't mind about this!) If you feel that this is challenging to do, consider singing along to audio or video as a 'scaffold'.
- Initiate and join in with action songs such as 'The Grand Old Duke of York' or 'Five Little Ducks'. Change the words to include the children's names and use objects or other children to represent the soldiers or the ducks!
- Enlist children's help to dig, weed and plant. You can introduce new language as you talk about what you are doing as you are doing it, such as 'trowel', 'hoe', 'seedlings', 'bulb'. Ask open-ended questions about what they think is needed for a plant to grow and what they think will happen next.
- Introduce singing to children as a fun and engaging activity that you can learn together. Look out for free resources and training that you can access online such as https://www.makaton.org/

In summary

- All theorists agree that children are born with the capabilities to learn language and the ability to communicate intention to others.
- Sociocultural constructivists (Vygotsky and Bruner) believe that it is the social and cultural context (the people, environment and objects) that scaffolds language learning.
- Chomsky argues that language acquisition is led by a built-in biological mechanism that needs 'switching' on by the environment – a nativist approach.
- As children play, they use multiple modes of communication to extend their representation of ideas to others.
- Language play and singing with babies and young children as an extension of a loving relationship helps them to learn about who they are in the world and provides them with foundational literacy skills and knowledge.

Having read this chapter, here are some **discussion questions** to help you plan young children's language and communication play:

1. How do you/would you organise a play environment (the spaces, people and materials) so that young children are encouraged to describe and represent their ideas to others using multiple modes of communication?

2. Consider how you have communicated with babies and toddlers in the past. How would you develop intersubjectivity with infants in the future?

Further recommended reading

Meyer. R. J. and Whitmore. K. F. (Eds.) (2016) *Reclaiming Early Childhood Literacies: Narratives of Hope, Power, and Vision*. Abingdon, Routledge.

This book has brought together a range of different writers – researchers as well as teachers – to highlight the possibilities of young children's multimodal literacies within the home, early years settings and school environments.

Saxton, M. (2017) *Child Language: Acquisition and Development* (2nd ed.). London: Sage.

Matthew Saxton's book provides a very thorough account of the development of children's language from a psychological perspective. It is really useful for extending your understanding of the theory sections in this chapter.

3

PLAYING NARRATIVELY: STORIES, IMAGINATION AND ROLE PLAY

This chapter will

- develop your understanding of the link between narrative, role play and literacy;
- provide you with an understanding of how imaginative role play supports the knowledge and skills that underpin literacy;
- help you to recognise the best ways to support young children to be imaginative storytellers.

In the same way that play is a universal part of early childhood, explanatory and imaginative narratives are a universal part of human culture. How we express these narratives is most recognisably in the form of storytelling, often conveyed by children in diverse communicative modes: language, gesture, vocalisation, movement, mark-making, etc. We often think of stories contained in print; however, human cultures have rich histories of oral, pictorial and musical storytelling – consider, for example, the nursery rhymes, the sayings, the folk tales as well and the family 'stories' that you grew up with. Stories are also evident as a visual form, for example in film, children's shows and illustrated books. Stories have an incredible power over us as humans both in their re-telling as well as in the drive we have to invent new ones. Most of us would recognise the feverish desire to know what happens next in the cliff-hanger stories that we are invested in. And as we construct stories of ourselves for others to hear, the 'telling' we do helps us to make sense of our own lives. For children, the immersive qualities that stories have can be observed in their pretend play – the dressing up, acting, and use of objects in novel ways – which are all born out of a desire to make-up and share a story.

In this chapter, we make links between narrative, stories and literacies, showing that by supporting young children to be storytellers we are enabling them to become authors. We will also consider how adults can best support young children to create rich and fulfilling stories, by observing carefully or being play participants themselves. We will look at how young children make and create stories by merging together both imaginative and real-life experiences as they play alone or together. Their vignette below is a good illustration of this, as it shows that by taking on real-life roles and using their imagination children employ different literacies to extend their play. Note how productive the children are as they borrow narratives from their real life experience to solve complex problems and continue the storytelling play.

┤Vignette├

Storytelling possibilities in joint exploratory play

A group of four Reception children are playing as construction workers on a building site. They have been engaged for most of the morning moving sand and mud using the collection of toy vehicles that they borrowed from the classroom. At the top of the slope is a sandpit and at the bottom of the slope a place for digging mud. The slope forms the track between the two, and the 'construction work' that they have agreed between them involves moving sand from the top to the bottom of the slope and mud from the bottom to the top using various toy vehicles that have been gathered.

After a while, the small group of children, in their hard hats and fluorescent jackets, crouch down at the bottom of the slope outside of their classroom, peering at the dumper truck that has crashed into the wall of the next-door classroom, spilling sand onto the path. They discuss what happened and why the vehicle may have spun out of control. They talk about the possibilities that might explain why it crashed into the wall: whether it was pushed too hard, whether it was pointing in the right direction, whether it had too much sand in it. They accept that while it is difficult to know, they do agree that it was going too fast to stop it in time. One child offers that they, 'haven't seen this happen on the building site near to where they live and the dumper trucks there are filled up really high'. After further observations about building sites are shared, a site manager is appointed. She states that she needs to have a clipboard and paper and she eagerly disappears to ask her teacher whether she can borrow one. After a few minutes, she reappears with the requisite clipboard, paper and pen and proceeds to gather everyone together to record their names and their jobs. She lists the workers' names down one side of the page and their assigned jobs next to their name: 'digger', 'builder', 'emptier', 'in charge'. There is some disagreement and discussion about who wants to do what before the children agree to swap some roles around, and the play resumes.

The significance of narrative

The way children construct knowledge of the world is sometimes likened to computation. Children's brains it is argued, as the centre of thinking, work like a computer: data is entered, processed, stored and then retrieved when necessary.

Files get bigger, and new files are created in response to new stimulus. We can see this model applied to how learning is often understood and measured in schools – as a process of building memory, or capacity to hold and sort data, and then systematically apply the stored information when needed. However appealing, computational approaches to learning are simplistic and misleading. The vignette above highlights the complex processes that underlie young children's learning, where materials, bodies, spaces, and importantly for this chapter, experience and imagination come together.

Bruner (1991) provides us with an explanation of how humans construct reality, giving us a more detailed understanding of how young children think; one that explains the complexities of storytelling play. He primarily focuses on the mind and the social environment, rather than bodies and materials; however, he recognises the intricacies of thought, as well as the contradictions that occur as part of thinking – the raking back and forth between the present, past and potential future (González-Monteagudo, 2011). Bruner argues that what shapes children's thinking is narrative, a narrative formed through the social and cultural sharing of common knowledge and stories between people. Children learn the common features of their 'cultural stories' including their patterns and discourses (the social practices and ways of communicating them), and this occurs through their everyday encounters and actions (Smidt, 2006).

Narratives, Bruner claims, are temporal (related to a sequence of time or of a particular time) and often chronological (moving in a time linear direction). Encouragingly, narratives aren't fixed and given, but are embellished, diminished or extended as children engage with them. As narrative thinkers, children are therefore placed in an agentive position as they can change their narratives and influence the narratives of others as 'actors' in a shared story. By positioning children as thinkers who construct their own narratives of the world, Bruner (1986) recognised the creative possibilities that narrative thought has, and the potential children have for constructing other worlds. Young children's play, with its essential open-ended and exploratory features, is a perfect way for children to construct other narrative worlds; they do this by transforming materials, spaces and the tools of language as a process of story making. When young children play together, they are encouraged to be both story listeners and storytellers with the capacity to make their imagined stories real.

As highlighted, the process of engaging in a narrative enables the child to be an interpreter of events and a driver of change. A child's role in forming a narrative is to be a cultural improvisor and creator of new possibilities in order to move the story forward. In doing this, they will draw on certain 'narrative moves' related to shared stories that they already know. As examples, in the story of Cinderella there are some constant narrative moves in how the story is told, for instance there is always a lost shoe and a prince; without these moves we couldn't necessarily describe the story as the 'Cinderella' story. And in stories about going to the shops, there will always be something to buy, and a way of getting there. If stories were retold with just their narrative moves, they would be very predictable and unexciting, but luckily, they also involve creative features, or 'colour moves', and these affect how the story is told, providing depth and interest. This is where child's agency – their ability to affect changes to the story – comes to the fore. Colour moves are the child's way of elaborating on the narrative and importantly are where the imaginative qualities of storytelling lies; it is where the excitement comes alive in thinking of new things that will happen next. It can be observed when children use different voices, add plot developments and characters, and select and use objects in creative ways. Children build both narrative moves and colour into their stories by drawing on past experience; juxtaposing the acknowledged structure of events and their imagination. This improvisation is an essentially playful process and when observed involves deep levels of concentration, quick-wittedness and emotional investment.

Reflection

Think about the last time you told a friend about an event that happened to you. Did you colour your own narrative by embellishing the events, adding gestures or certain phrases? Did the added colour make your story funnier, more thought provoking, or dramatic? How did your friend's response encourage your telling of the story?

Storytelling

Bruner claimed that speech is an essential feature of narrative. He argued that the everyday speech between children and their carers is driven by a sense of shared story-making. The descriptions of events, the choice of words and gestures, all go towards the development of shared meaning making. These narratives, based on shared language, occur as part of our everyday life, and guide children to recognise how to produce successful interactions. Language and particularly speech help us to create 'our' stories of family, friendships and play and both adults and children have a part to play in carefully listening to, and assembling, these shared stories. As Tim Ingold (2011, p. 162) writes,

> A person who can 'tell' is one who is perpetually attuned to picking up information in the environment ... and the teller, in rendering his knowledge explicit, conducts the attention of his audience along the same paths as his own.

Vivian Gussin Paley wrote in *The Boy Who Would be a Helicopter* that, 'amazingly children are born knowing how to put every thought and feeling into story form'

(1990, p. 4). In her many observations of young children's storytelling, Paley (1990, 1992, 2004) provides us with fascinating accounts of the power of young children's fantasy play as a vehicle for their learning. She also explores her own role as a 'connection maker' for the children, as she fosters, revisits and reviews their stories, helping children to associate what they do with what other storytellers and authors do. Paley describes play as 'story in action', and like Bruner, that 'storytelling is play put into a narrative form' (1990, p. 4). She explains that stories help to structure and organise the random features of play as the 'bridges built in play are lengthened, their partially exposed signposts organised and labelled in ways that commit the storyteller to travel in particular directions' (1990, p. 35).

Young children use stories as a way to arrange and order, through the use of objects and language, what they know as well as what it is possible to imagine. The stories they tell, whether they act them out, speak them, or write or draw them, are a way for them to share their thinking. Paley tells her own story of how she listens to children's stories by stepping into the 'rhythm' that they inhabit. Storytelling, she argues, is a way for children to build culture as they are told to a participatory audience, encouraging shared meaning making for all involved.

Paley's work has led to a pedagogical practice known as 'Helicopter Stories' (Lee, 2016), which have helped educators recognise the key features needed to maximise storytelling opportunities for young children. This approach foregrounds the theatrical nature of storytelling and story-listening. The child/children decide the parts they want to play, and then they act out their story on the stage (a taped-off area of the classroom). The practitioner listens to the child/children and transcribes their stories word for word. This is a carefully arranged and scaffolded process, although there is a question about who is doing the scaffolding, the child or the adult? Helicopter Stories as a pedagogical practice helps children to solve dramatic problems, echoing their real-life challenges, but in a safe environment. Young children are given the opportunity to rehearse possible realities; the good and the bad, the mundanities of life as well as the excitements, the harmless aspects of life together with the dangerous. Hugely important in this practice is the control the children have in being able to tell their story and the role of the practitioner in making sure all children's voices are heard. It reinforces the link between the spoken and the written word, and is based on a notion of respect for others and value given to the voices of the children involved.

Storytelling between adults and children is a common occurrence in the familial relationships formed at home. Smeed's (2012) observations of the process of constructing imaginative stories with her two-year-old nephew Noah, demonstrated how an adult can get into the rhythm of a child's storytelling so that they can become a play partner. Smeed recognised that although she couldn't fully know what was in her nephew's imagination, she had an important role as a listener and supporter of joint meaning making, describing her job as being an 'effective props mistress' (p. 7). She also noted that the emotions Noah demonstrated during his play helped him process his feelings. Having listened rather than steered Noah's story-making, Smeed was able to respond to his humour and interests successfully by introducing new characters, different plot lines and carnivalesque language that subverted the routine and predictable forms of language use.

Drawing on Froebelian principles of play (see Chapter 1), a group of Scottish practitioner-enquirers have recently shown how storytelling activities are a way of connecting together the child's sense of self and their relationships with others, including their wider community (Bruce et al., 2020). These projects often began with the sharing of a traditional story – drawing on cultural practices of oral story-telling in Scotland – chosen because of their cross-cultural themes and values. Their work with the children details a variety of storytelling activities in each setting including puppetry, woodland adventures, superhero role play and animation. In reflecting on their work, the practitioners talk about the need for close observation that can bring a deeper level of understanding of each child's language and ideas, in order to 'tune into what it feels like to be a child' (Imray and Clements, 2020, p. 14). There is also a recognition in their work that children's narratives can be seen, not only when they are staged and performed, but also in the quieter moments of play, often beginning with small events that can build and expand.

Reflection

When you are playing with children, how do you interact with them so that they can rehearse their ideas? How do you tune into the 'rhythm' of their storytelling?

Pretend and small world play

Miniature worlds have always had a fascination for children, offering them a child-sized realm through which to direct events. Small world play provides young children with a world where they have control and can assert agency over the environment and carry huge potential in providing immersive play experiences. As well as being tactile and easily held, small objects are able to be carried around and so are therefore both transportable and adaptable (remember a narrative must move). By bringing together a combination of both manufactured toys (e.g. fairies, dinosaurs, figures, animals, trains and cars) and natural or multi-use materials (e.g. shells, stones and blocks) children can create fantastical worlds. These worlds can involve a multitude of inhabitants and habitats, some more fixed to real life, or socio-dramatic play (e.g. doll's houses, farms and train tracks) and others which are more fantasy based (e.g. fairy pocket-sized grottos and trolls).

The key to small world play is pretence. As the real-life size of objects is disturbed, the play immediately starts with a suspension of 'truth'; an imaginative space that provides them with the capacity to think through stories (Bruner, 1986; Egan, 1986). As Smidt writes, 'in pretend play, the child stimulates an action in play as if it were real, or the child tries out new combinations and consequences in a "what if" fashion' (2006, p. 46). The features of pretence also offer children with a strategy for excluding and resisting adult agendas and governance, and empowering their own cultural practices (Grieshaber and McArdle, 2010).

Bateman (2018) in her research highlights the central feature of ventriloquism as part of pretend play. She writes that pretend play involves, 'playing out an impromptu storyline where ventriloquism is used to talk objects into life through paralinguistic features such as gesture, gaze and voice prosody' (2018, p. 68). Bateman argues that when children speak the voice of the characters, either alone or with others, they are engaging in complex meaning-making processes where they orally formulate characters and build coherent and systematic storylines. It is useful to consider how adults are able to enhance and extend these features of pretend play.

The case study below illustrates how Vicky's grandmother subtly enhanced and extended her pretend play.

Case Study

Enhancing and Extending Storytelling

Four-year-old Vicky is lying on her front on the floor of her grandparents' living room. Her grandmother Jane is used to Vicky helping herself to the castle and small fairies that she keeps in her under stairs cupboard. They were Vicky's mother's toys and whenever Vicky visits, she always makes her way straight to this cupboard, lifts out the miniature castle and takes in into the living room where she proceeds to set up the castle people: fairies and witches, in various positions, depending on today's ideas for her story.

Jane has noticed through quietly observing her granddaughter, that the stories usually revolve around popular fairy tales that involve good fairies and bad fairies and witches that are always bad. She wants to encourage the development of her granddaughter's imagination so today she decides to try changing the narrative. She introduces the treasures that they acquired on their earlier walk in the woods – stones, sticks, leaves and acorns – into the play scenario by piling them onto a small cart accompanied by a horse that she found when clearing out her daughter's old toys the previous week. As she plays alongside Vicky, she states that they are 'witches' treasure' and that they are full of good spells. She empties the cart next to the witch nearby and waits to see what Vicky does next.

(Continued)

> To her delight, Vicky takes the bait and changes her usual story from one that is centred on the fairies as good and the witches as bad, instead picking up the witch character, and declaring 'abracadabra, now you are a good witch' before voicing aloud the fairies' response; 'now you are good, you are allowed to come into my castle'. Jane's gentle prompting has subtly influenced the play and challenged Vicky's ideas of who is 'allowed' to be good and bad, thus empowering Vicky to consider alternative scenarios.

Reflective questions

How does Jane encourage different narratives in Vicky's imaginative play?

What is the impact of Jane's role in Vicky's imaginative storytelling?

Playing in role

Vygotsky (2004) argued that the significance of role play lies in how it operates as a social experience. Construction of new knowledge is able to take place through the social exchange between children and their playmates or adult/carers as they take on different and diverse roles. Smilansky and Shefataya (1990) highlight the difference between dramatic play, where children act out an imaginative scenario alone and the focus is on play objects (see small world play above), and socio-dramatic play, where children play together and the focus shifts to people (see the vignette at the start of this chapter).

Importantly, as children act out a role they are forced to think differently, and this challenges them to hypothesise about what the world could be (Cremin et al., 2017). It is a process of questioning and disrupting, as alternative ways of acting and doing things are introduced to stimulate new ways of critically thinking about the world (Kingdon, 2020). It is through this critical questioning that young children are able to create fictional and imaginative worlds to inhabit, mapping these creative possibilities onto their own experience and stretching their understanding of how it is possible to think, feel and act. Taking on a different role, or being situated in another 'place', encourages children to see things from another perspective, creating a leap in imagination and empathy through the feelings associated with being both 'inside' and 'outside' of the role they are playing (Fleer, 2018a). The development of imagination and the ability to envision possibilities and potential – a central feature of acting in role – is one of the reasons that role play is so important in supporting literacy, as possibility thinking is necessary for reading and text creation (Cremin et al., 2013).

However, the potential of young children's imaginative role play is framed by inequalities. Children's role play is often limited to previous experiences, the language they have encountered through everyday interactions, and the resources that they have available to them. Bodrova and Leong (2003) have argued that children from socioeconomically disadvantaged backgrounds engage in lower levels of socio-dramatic play as a consequence of having fewer play materials and less space to play in. Young children may also have limited cultural experiences to stimulate a diversity of roles within their play (Corsaro, 2003; Scrafton and Whitington, 2015), although the roles that children are familiar with may be misunderstood and devalued due to cultural preferences. Alongside this, some educational settings, despite valuing children's play as a way of developing imagination, may be missing opportunities to be fully involved in children's role play so as to extend its potential. Devi et al.'s (2018) research, for example, showed that even though practitioners were very good at asking children questions, observing them, and acting as narrators as well as providing materials for role play, they rarely acted and played alongside children as play partners.

Adults and children making stories together

Young children are amazingly resourceful in leading their own imaginative role play and often need little organising from adults to keep the play moving along. Sensitive practitioners are conscious of acting in a way that may risk interrupting the flow of children's play; however, adults who 'play along' can expand imaginative play in their conversations with children as co-players, as well as by introducing materials to enrich the event. Children bring rich and diverse experiences of their home language and culture, as well as their media experiences into their play, and this should be valued and encouraged. In order to overcome social and material inequalities that potentially restrict children's stories, practitioners should do their best to extend the cultural, social and material resources of children's play to represent the many diverse realities in our society as well as imagined alternatives. If adults bring 'themselves' into imaginative play with children they can pass on their own knowledge of different roles, characters and scenarios, and extend children's language use.

Researchers have shown the benefits of playing alongside children to extend their imagination and planning of role-play ideas. In extensive observations of socially advantaged and disadvantaged children, psychologist Sara Smilansky (1968) was one of the first to show that adult intervention strategies, or play-tutoring as she referred to it, increased children's engagement benefiting less advantaged children. She advocated adults using modelling techniques, asking children questions, discussing their ideas with them and selecting exciting materials for their play. Scrafton and Whitington (2015) recommend that educators support disadvantaged children in their socio-dramatic play by providing explicit language and social support within a stimulating physical environment, specifically to help shy, and culturally and linguistically challenged children. Lobman (2003) also showed that training practitioners in the skills of improvisation resulted in the extension of dramatic possibilities and the development of complex plots and conversation in young children's role play. Gupta (2009), while recognising the necessity of child initiation, advocates adult direction of role play as a way of maximising the processes involved in joint meaning making. This interaction, where adults are sharing tools for storying, can help children to make sense of their ideas. From this, the adult and the child are able to create shared playworlds (Lindqvist, 1995).

Building literacy through imaginative play

As we have shown, imaginary play in all its many forms nurtures children's use of more advanced language related to certain scenarios or social roles, encouraging language and vocabulary growth (Pellegrini, 1984). We can see in the vignette at the start of this chapter that when adults provide dressing up outfits and organise time and space for dramatic play it stimulates children to practise functional uses of language, as well as literacy in context (Weisberg et al., 2013). Importantly, the capacity of children to engage in imaginary play is a predictor of their literacy abilities as they move into more formal learning environments (Nicolopoulou et al., 2006). Longitudinal studies have shown that the quality of four to five-year-olds' socio-dramatic and imaginary play predicts their performance on standardised tests of narrative competence three to five years later (Stagnitti and Lewis, 2015). Evidence also shows that by participating in organised regular storytelling and socio-dramatic play programmes, young children improve their language use, literacy and self-regulation abilities (Nicolopoulou et al., 2015). It is therefore how imaginative play is organised as a regular, participatory event, and the qualities that this then fosters, that affects the extent to which it supports literacy.

Importantly, imaginative play is linked to literacy because of the symbolic use of objects, people and spaces to represent and transform what is 'real'. These acts encourage young children to understand symbolic representation (Engel, 2005), helping them to grasp the idea that letters and numerals can also be symbolic of sounds, and when combined can symbolise words and formulas that have meaning. This symbolic action also encourages children to share diverse stories from their cultural heritage that have different genres and characters, increasing children's awareness that there are different types of story forms (Flynn, 2018).

Being in role allows children to have a tangible experience of how characters move, speak, behave and feel, and this can be transferred into other literate forms such as written stories (CLPE, n.d). The elements of drama necessary within role play provide a way for children to investigate possible fictional scenarios and explore the implications of actions, all of which fosters detailed imaginative story writing (Dombey, 2013). Children have power of authorship in dramatic play, and this authorship is increased by having their stories written down by an adult and read aloud to others. This scribing process helps familiarise children with writing and its uses in a concrete and engaging way (Nicolopoulou et al., 2006).

If we take a broader view of literacy as multimodal and material, as well as social and cognitive, imaginative play also offers children a way of engaging in literate processes of design and production. Flewitt (2017) has shown that by examining the integrated multimodal aspects of storytelling (movement, gaze and speech) of children with English as a second language the strengths within each child's communication practices can be recognised. Flewitt has demonstrated that in storytelling practices such as Helicopter Stories approach discussed previously young children who may find speaking in a classroom situation a challenge, are given space to have their ideas and interests heard and scribed; helping them to gain confidence and recognising their unique capabilities. She argues that the centrality of multimodality within storytelling provides a more inclusive curriculum that values linguistic and cultural diversity through the multiple modes of expression that are encouraged.

Focusing on the importance of space and materials, Wohlwend's (2011, 2013) research has looked at the effect that the incorporation of 'literacy playshops' into early childhood settings has on young children's text making. Starting from the perspective that children's literate practices are socio-materially constructed, Wohlwend's playshops foster pretend play and imagination as part of a cooperative process from which to create a shared 'script'. These scripts may be written, performed or drawn or animated. Playshops are transient spaces negotiated by the children and teachers, not fixed to one area, allowing for the fluidity and improvisation necessary for narratives to function. Wohlwend argues that this approach encourages young children to extend their ideas about literacy by combining different materials and features of literacy in imaginative ways. The playshop approach allows children to produce rich cultural texts that draw on their cultural experience of music, drama, popular media and other art forms, and incorporate multilingual and diverse visual features (Wohlwend, 2013).

The following case study illustrates how Jamal fosters his children's experiences and imagination to enable them to cooperatively create shared scripts though a playshop approach.

Case Study

Developing Shared Scripts Through the Use of Materials

Jamal is a preschool practitioner. He does all he can to enable the children in his setting to access the outdoor environment; however, this is challenging because he works in a pack-away preschool and the immediate outdoor space consists of a fenced-off tarmac area next to the local park. Jamal has noticed that the children particularly enjoy sand and water play and lately, he has heard one of the other practitioners complaining about the children mixing these. He discusses this with her explaining how he remembers his own experiences as a child, spending hours mixing mud and water in his garden and considers that mixing materials is beneficial as children can explore and talk about their properties, learning new descriptive words in the process. The practitioner agrees and together they discuss Jamal's idea of setting up a 'kitchen playshop' where children could go to 'buy' their ingredients to mix for their recipes and make pretend food for their toys. They encourage the children to discuss and share their ideas for the shop, including imagining the fantasy food that they could create. Next, they ask for suggestions of what they could use to put the different ingredients in. One child suggests that they use some plastic boxes that are stacked in the shed as containers. The children respond enthusiastically to ideas for materials to put in the containers such as sand, mud, water, flour, pasta and rice. Another child suggests that they use old plastic bottles as 'scoops' (like their dad does for dog biscuits). They collect all of the empty containers they can find along with a till and weighing scales to set the shop up. The playshop is complete and the children are excited to begin playing with it. Jamal plays with the children in being a customer and suggesting 'mixtures', he asks them for ideas of what to call the mixtures and who will be coming to the shop. Jamal tells them about his mud kitchen experiences as a child and all sorts of creative language and stories emerge as they mix the ingredients together.

Reflective questions

How did Jamal extend the children's imagination and storytelling through his actions?

Do you agree that this is an important learning experience that required support?

What did the children learn from being included in making decisions about how to organise the different materials?

As we have discussed, young children have a brilliant natural capacity for storytelling, and adults have an important role in supporting young children to maximise this potential through a combination of direction, resourcing and, most importantly, listening in order to value what children are saying in their play. That means being part of, not separate from, their flights of imagination. As Vivien Gussin Paley remarks,

> If I am to step to the rhythm of the storytellers who inhabit my classroom, I must perform on their stage or we will seldom hear one another. (1990, p. 7)

Practice ideas

The following ideas may be useful in supporting children's storytelling and imaginative play:

- Make your own puppet theatre by recycling cardboard boxes and scraps of fabric. Involve the children in deciding how to make puppets from materials in the classroom/setting. Encourage the children to give their puppet a name and character (what does their character like to eat, play with and watch on screen?). You might consider beginning the play with a provocation, e.g. one of the characters has got lost, or an event, e.g. a birthday party. Join in the play with your own puppet and character and gently prompt the children to solve problems and provide them with possible storylines. Ask 'what for', 'why' and 'how' questions to help the children express their opinions and observations. You might even rehearse the story and video it to share with family and friends.
- Create a socio-dramatic role-play area that reflects the real-life experience of children in the class, e.g. a shop or a vet, or extend children's cultural experiences by creating a theatre, celebration or a holiday resort. Provide prompts, props, costumes digital devices, writing materials, books and pictures to help stimulate the play. As you play with the children, be curious and ask them open questions (e.g. tell me more about that, or what do you think about this?). Encourage children to label, describe, and explain objects or actions in their play.
- Cover a space in the classroom/setting with white material or paper (you could use a roll of wallpaper on the floor). Collect small world animals and figures as well as natural found material such as pebbles, twigs and leaves. Encourage children to draw maps, roads, paths, and other geographical features of their story, as well as signs and instructions on the material or paper as they play. Ask the children to name the places and characters they are creating. Suggest funny names and voices to help extend the storyline as well as the enjoyment, e.g. 'Flubber-lubber land', 'Marshall big pants rabbit' or 'Flying stick boy'.

In summary

- Children make sense of their social, cultural and material world (and who they are within it) through shared cultural stories.
- Storytelling allows children to engage in possibility thinking, or 'what if' scenarios which help extend thinking and tool use.
- Children are able to create 'narratives' or stories by changing ideas, moving between spaces and adapting materials.
- Young children should be encouraged to engage in a wide range of storytelling practices including small world and socio-dramatic play as this enhances their language and multimodal literacy practices.
- Adults should recognise the diverse cultural stories that children bring into the classroom/setting and support all children by encouraging regular storytelling activities and playing alongside them, introducing characters, plot and extending their vocabulary.

Having read this chapter, here are some **discussion questions** to help you in planning for young children's storytelling, imagination and role-play experiences:

1. What materials do you think are needed in order to create a rich storytelling environment for young children? Where should these materials be placed in the classroom/setting? Who should have access and when should they be able to use them?

2. Are there types of imaginative play that you like or dislike? Why do you think you have a preference? How do you manage these preferences so that all children are able to play imaginatively in your setting?

Further recommended reading

Bruce, T., McNair, L. and Whinnett, J. (Eds.) (2020) *Putting Storytelling at the Heart of Early Childhood Practice.* Abingdon, Routledge.

This book has been written by participants of the Edinburgh Froebel Network (as mentioned above), many of whom work as early years leaders and practitioners. It will spark lots of your own ideas as it provides vibrant examples of practice in supporting and observing children's pretend play and storytelling, including work with props and superhero play.

Cremin, T., Flewitt, R., Mardell, B. and Swann, J. (Eds.) (2017) *Storytelling in Early Childhood: Enriching Language, Literacy and Classroom Culture.* Abingdon, Routledge.

This book contains chapters by many key researchers in the field of storytelling and early literacy providing further insight into the importance of storytelling as a corner stone of literacy.

4

MAKING A MARK ON THE WORLD: PLAYFUL WRITING

┌─ **This chapter will** ─┐

- help you understand the connection between mark-making, writing and young children's play;
- introduce you to theories that explain how, and why, children make marks and play with symbols;
- highlight the significance of materials and objects in children's mark-making and writing;
- provide you with a case study – 'The Playful writing project' – to show you how play can support young children's writing.

This chapter focuses on play's unique capacity to facilitate young children's mark-making and writing. When children engage in intense and purposeful play, they often want to symbolise what they are doing through real or virtual marks on different surfaces. In the previous chapters, we showed how children are agentic in pursuing language and communication with others. This desire to communicate and 'say something' extends into their use of mark-making, drawing and writing tools as well. Play environments, where different material resources are readily available and can be used creatively, enable children to symbolise their thinking and communication, encouraging them to make marks and use written symbols. Researchers (Hall and Robinson, 2003; Wohlwend, 2008) have shown that there is a symbiotic relationship between writing and play. Children draw and write in order to pursue and sustain their play, and symbolic mark-making also has a role in extending children's potential to play. We will look at this in more detail in the case study at the end of this chapter.

To help you understand further how the foundations of writing are fostered within children's play consider the vignette below – an observation of a child who is simultaneously playing and writing in an early years school setting. The two elements are woven together; the writing is part of the child's play, and the play is part of the child's writing. As you read, consider how the writing is being produced as part of the play. Think also about how the child's writing is changing the shape of the play.

━ Vignette ━

Composing writing in role play

Charlie (four years old) is playing with another child at being post office/delivery people. They each wear a cap and have made badges with their names on from stickers. Charlie has a clipboard with paper and pencil attached and writes down the deliveries by listing ticks, crosses and letters in columns on the page to show that the things have been delivered. He negotiates the workload of the deliveries and collections with the other child telling him what he is writing down and pointing across the classroom to where things should be delivered. He marks the paper with squiggles and ticks, arranged in different places, talking and gesturing all the time to his playmate. Pretty soon it is tidying-up time, and Charlie's play is interrupted by the speedy movements of other children, who squeeze past him while they reach over to put things back into trays and balance stuff on shelves. Charlie starts to argue with his classmates, telling them not to touch his clipboard. He doesn't want to stop his 'work'. Eventually he relents, but rather than putting the clipboard in its assigned space in the writing area, he pushes it down the side of a nearby cupboard so that it became wedged against the wall and can't be seen by anyone else. In the following weeks, Charlie goes back to where the clipboard is, and uses it within his play either with others or alone, carefully sliding it back into its hiding space whenever he is interrupted.

The observation shows Charlie to be deeply engrossed in his play, so much so that he is resistant to the requests of others. It could be that his actions as a writer immerse him further into his imaginary world, a world he doesn't want to leave behind. The vignette also shows us how important writing objects can be for children; like many adult writers, the tools child writers engage with have significant meaning making potential. This 'preciousness' of mark-making and writing materials will be explored further as you read through this chapter.

Multimodal authorship

When Charlie is 'writing' in the vignette above, he does this alongside other modes of communication: drawing, speech, gesture, body movements, etc. As we know from the multimodal approaches outlined in Chapter 2, children's early literacy is an overlapping ensemble of modes of communication. Mavers (2011, p. 6) explains that it is an 'embodied, not just "mindful" experience', meaning that it is an experience where the physical act of doing it is inextricably linked to the child's perception and meaning-making process (Merleau-Ponty, 2002). We need to be careful not to ignore crucial elements in the production of these symbolic marks. If you observe children's writing you will know that a child's movements, their gaze and gestures, the tone and cadence of their voice and the words they are speaking are all important aspects in how their writing is 'made'. The production of writing needs to be observed alongside all the other aspects of communication that help it into fruition, this may include drawing and talking, bodily movement, even humming and singing. To motivate young children to be literacy producers we need to be good at recognising all of these elements and valuing them. So, encourage children to use a range of communication modes and movement while they make marks and write, as this will aid their thinking as well as their creative engagement in making it.

The physicality of mark-making

As stated above, mark-making, drawing and writing are embodied experiences. Children need to develop sophisticated awareness of their body and how it moves to be able to successfully create the shapes and marks they want. These activities take an enormous amount of physical dexterity, involving gross motor control of the shoulder and arm and core strength, so that the child can move into comfortable positioning (Cowley, 2019). For children to develop skill and accuracy in their mark-marking and the confident control of tools and materials, fine movement of hands and fingers, as well as secure posture are needed for comfort and fluency. Children also need to be able to focus their vision on what they are physically doing and track marks on a page – hand–eye coordination. Children's abilities as drawers and writers will increase through a range of opportunities provided to strengthen their physicality. The correct dynamic tripod grasp to hold a pen or pencil, commonly referred to as the pincer grip, should not be rushed but follow on from lots of experience of fine motor activities such as bead threading and block play, as this will support the underpinning physical and visual development needed for confident tool use.

The importance of materials

Children store great importance in the materials and objects they use in mark-making and writing. A child said to us once, '…with this Batman pen I can write about Batman…'. This set us off wondering how he thought writing worked. What the child was expressing (quite firmly!) was that it was the pen itself that provided him with his particular writing 'abilities'. These abilities came about through the pen's usage, as well as the media associations assigned to it. The pen represented the actual content (about Batman) that could be transposed into writing. What was significant, therefore, was the pen's material make-up – its batman shape and colour – as these elements affected the sensation he had of using it. Thinking about this and considering the opening vignette again, if Charlie had been writing on a clean sheet of A4 would it have been the same writing experience for him? Charlie's prized clipboard clearly had a special 'energy' that allowed him to do something worth keeping hidden. Bennett (2010) would argue that for Charlie and the child with the Batman pen, the objects they are using have a material 'vibrancy'; the same agentic quality that living things have. The source of the child's actions as a writer comes from the relationship that exists between the child and the material object: the pen or the clipboard.

The anthropologist Tim Ingold suggests that humans shape culture and humanity through practices of inhabitation within, and as part of, the material world. Children make things by being immersed in the material world that they have access to. Ingold in his examination of human mark-making across cultures emphasises the practice of doing: making, creating, storying, drawing, writing. In other words, human action. Mark-making, drawing and writing are all states of action in the world, part of human existence as 'materials confront the creative imagination' (Ingold, 2011, p. 23). When children make a mark on paper with a crayon, use a finger to tap a screen, or scratch the sand with a stick they are exploring the potential of these materials – the multiple possibilities that can be produced when they play with them.

As Barad has explained in an interview with Juelskjaer and Schwennesen (2021), we can describe children's engagement with materials when they are mark-making as 'intra-activity', a mingling of themselves, the objects (chalks, pens, brushes, sticks, straws, etc.) and a surface on which to place marks. The materials used are important as they help to construct the drawing or writing itself. These ideas challenge us to think more carefully about children's experience of materials differently and ask us to question the relationship between children's literacy and the objects used in literacy creation. Kuby et al.'s (2015) research of children's writing explored these questions and noted that children's use of materials or artefacts weren't pre-planned but 'unfolded' in the moments that the children were using them. The children's writing activity was made more desirable and expansive through their engagement with the materials on offer, their communication therefore inseparable from their material entanglements. This suggests that adults may be limiting the potential of writing objects and materials if they assign pre-determined usage of them for children. Play, as a less regulated activity, has the potential to open up the material possibilities of writing.

Reflection

Can you remember the drawing and writing objects you played with as a child? What were your favourite drawing and writing tools? Why were they so special?

Is it mark-making, drawing or writing?

We have described what Charlie is doing in the vignette above as writing, but it could also be described as mark-making or perhaps even drawing. It is useful to distinguish between these different modes of communication as they are assigned different social usage and value in early years settings and schools, affecting how children are introduced to them and how they view their potential as 'ways' of communicating to others. It is also important to recognise that when children engage with mark-making, drawing and writing in play situations they do so multimodally; often bringing the features of each together rather than separating them out, so that they can communicate with others in the most effective way.

Mark-making

Mark-making is a term grounded in the visual arts. The Tate Gallery (n.d., para 1) describes it as,

> the different lines, dots, marks, patterns, and textures we create ... it can be loose and gestural or controlled and neat. It can apply to any material used on any surface: paint on canvas, ink or pencil on paper, a scratched mark on plaster, a digital paint tool on a screen, a tattooed mark on skin ... even a sound can be a form of mark-making.

Ingold describes human mark-making as the tracings of manual gestures created as a continuous movement, by dragging or pulling of an implement (2007, p. 120). When children are mark-making, for example by painting with brushes on foil, or printing onto wet sand, they are creating lines or tracings on solid surfaces with technologies (tools) and their bodies.

Children's early mark-making activity is sometimes described as a 'pre-literate' activity as very young children may not be aware that marks 'carry' meanings and the marks they make do not symbolise formal literacy codes. In early years education it is often viewed as a precursor to writing as it helps children to develop writing 'skills' and although it may not be recognisable as writing it has potential as a representative act both for written language and number (PACEY, n.d.). Mark-making is therefore traditionally understood as a stage towards the development of formal writing. However, we need to be careful not to undermine children's engagement in mark-making activity as merely a stepping stone towards something more significant. Very young children's mark-making, as a foundational element of literacy, helps us to understand how language and communication tools are used within the process of writing, providing us with a useful insight into how literacy works with older children too.

John Matthews' research into young children's early mark-making as well as primate behaviours highlights the intentionality that lies behind young children's marks, arguing that these are never random acts. Matthews states that, 'Scribbles are products of a systematic investigation rather than haphazard actions' (1999, p. 19). Furthermore, Carruthers and Worthington's (2006) study examining 700 samples of young children's mark-making, showed how these representational 'graphics' supported the thinking processes necessary for the evolvement of recognisable forms of writing and mathematics. Bruce (2015) has also argued that young children's mark-making as something unique to who they are, signifies something deeply personal about themselves. Children's marks can, therefore, be viewed as having a purpose, conveying a sense of self, and representing meaning – they are symbolic of thought.

There are different perspectives on children's mark-making, however. Jolley (2010) argues that children engage in mark-making as a rewarding motor and sensory experience; it is the enjoyable feel of the material marks that is desirable for the child, rather than the need to 'say something'. It is the adult, rather than the very young child, that 'interprets' the marks as having representational meaning. Whitehead (2007) also notes how children are interested in the experimental nature of mark-making – how the speed and movement of the tool affects the mark – the potential it offers. These alternative views do not necessarily undermine mark-making as a process of signification – there is meaning for the child in the sensorial qualities of the flow of paint from the brush onto the smooth paper, or the flaky chalk on the hard concrete, but these 'movements' may not necessarily represent thinking, instead they can be understood through the affect that these materials have on children. Mark-making is symbolic, it does 'say something' to others that is intentional, but it is rooted in a material, embodied experience; all these elements are necessary to understand what is happening when children make marks and how best to support them to do this. The following example shows how a one-year-old child is enjoying making marks with food. This is often one of children's first mark-making experiences.

── ◖Vignette◗ ─────────────────────────────

Early explorations in meaningful mark-making

Ibrahim spills his yogurt onto the table at lunchtime and uses his finger to create a trail through it. He moves his finger quickly up and down and observes that it makes different marks to ones which go slowly from side to side. Ibrahim looks up at his carer and laughs. He continues to make marks with his whole hand making 'splat' noises as he slaps the table and occasionally licks the end of his fingers tentatively. He brings both hands into play and attempts to grab the yogurt from the table. His carer points to the marks he has made and Ibrahim follows her gaze looking intently at the imprints and patterns he has made.

Ibrahim may simply be enjoying the feeling and the movement of materials, but he is also creating meanings from this event as he explores what is possible from the materials he is playing with. Importantly, Ibrahim looks to others to get a response to what he is doing. The meanings of this early mark-making will come from the communication of others around them – how they acknowledge and share the experience by joining in, or talking about it. If the child understands that what they are doing is meaningful to others as well as themselves they will want to explore further by playing with more marks, more materials, and as a result applying more physical control.

Reflection

How much do you think young children's mark-making is about the feel and exploration of materials, or a desire to express something to someone else?

Drawing

Drawing and mark-making are often used simultaneously to describe the same type of activity in early years settings. The reason we look at drawing separately here is to highlight that it is often separated from mark-making. Mark-making is primarily viewed as a developmental stage in early childhood towards more formal literacy as described above, whereas drawing is viewed as a symbolic creative activity that children may become more skilled at, but do not grow out of. However, the difference is often blurred. What is significant is how practitioners and teachers understand the function it has as a mode of communication and its relationship to writing as a sign-making activity.

Lancaster's research (2007) based on the multimodal analysis of children under the age of three shows that children are aware of the differences between writing and drawing at a very young age and use graphic signs in their own mark-making. However, attempting to isolate drawing from writing for young children is futile as they do not operate within the same set of adult assumptions related to graphic systems. Writing and drawing are abstract terms for very young children. We can see this as children grow older too, in the sense that they are surrounded by visual as well as textual information and this is represented in the way in which they choose to communicate their ideas by mixing drawing and writing together on a page.

When young children enter formal schooling, drawing is viewed as quite a different type of activity to writing. It is associated less with literacy and more with creativity and, therefore, not measured or assessed in the same way. Like mark-making, there is evidence that drawing is seen merely as a 'stepping stone' in the development of writing, rather than an important process of communication in itself (Ring, 2006; Hall, 2009). The outcome of this is that the value of drawing is often downplayed in relation to more formalised language systems, devaluing the importance of it in terms of literacy. Children will learn the value associated with drawing through their social experiences and how it is organised for them in childhood settings. As children get older, drawing often goes unchecked by adults, whereas writing is carefully monitored and assessed as it has more value in terms of the literacy curriculum. Drawing is, therefore, unintentionally organised by adults into a more 'freeing' activity, often driven by the child's interests and taking place in less regulated learning spaces and has lots in common with some of the descriptions of play given in Chapter 1. Perhaps this is why children generally enjoy drawing as it is offered as having multiple, rather than restrictive possibilities, and is open to experimentation. This contrasts with more prescribed learning activities associated with writing that children may experience in more formal settings.

However, drawing like other forms of literacy involves creativity, symbolic communication and authorship. Drawing and writing are closely related modes that children bring together in their literacy making to create readable 'texts'. We know from observing children playing that they use writing symbols in their drawings and vice versa (even if they are proficient writers) as the process of drawing helps mediate thinking, and enhances the construction of the text to communicate certain ideas (Kress, 2003; Yamada-Rice, 2013). Children, like many communication experts, know that sometimes an image is more 'telling' (more communicative) than a word and that the best communication often involves images and words coming together. Therefore, to gauge a better understanding of young children's literacy we need to look closely at the selection and design process that is taking place when children create new communicative texts; how children are using drawing and writing together to make meaning as an ensemble of signifying activity (Kress, 2010).

Writing

Writing can be identified specifically through the use of formal symbols to represent language. It is important to recognise that as humans we have developed our skills as writers to articulate our varying human experience. For instance, humans write music, computer code, mathematical equations and 'text speak', as well as the type of academic formal writing you are reading now. All of these written languages require sophisticated understanding and application of codes and symbols in order to represent the ideas, feelings and imagination of the writer so that their meanings can be conveyed accurately. Like the act of reading, the act of writing involves complex mental processing that can change our neurological structures (James, 2010). When children write they often engage in a considerable reflective process; playing and experimenting with structure, form and content as they explore potential possibilities within language (Cremin and Myhill, 2012).

Vygotsky (1978) informs us that play has an important role in supporting the construction of literate thinking processes by increasing children's awareness of the potential that symbols have as a way of representing their ideas to others. Vygotsky described play, alongside gesture, speech and drawing as a first-order symbol system. This describes how children use objects, physical actions such as voice, as well as mark-making, to communicate and create primary meanings. Writing is a second-order symbol system. It works in a similar, but more complex way because children have to know that they can represent movement and speech through the use of a codified cultural script. To understand fully how writing works we need to recognise speech and gesture as an entry point (Vygotsky, 1978).

Gesture-based writing

Vygotsky wrote that 'gesture is a writing in the air and the written sign is very frequently simply a fixed gesture' (1997, p. 133). This foregrounding of gesture in terms of its potential as a 'writing' act acknowledges that both simple and more complex communication systems develop from a shared gaze. The meanings of the child's gesture come initially from their focus on objects (as they attempt to grasp and feel materials in their early life). Adults then make this external action a meaningful social communication by interacting with the child and interpreting meanings with them. Adults follow the direction of the child's gaze and eventually the child points, and watches for their 'point' to be acknowledged. Vygotsky described how this developmental process of physical gesturing and shared meaning making is extended through children's tool use onto different surfaces.

Children's writing is a similar process to pointing with a shared gaze, as the child is signifying objects and intentional direction as well as action, and this has social meaning to others (Dyson, 1993). The findings from Rowe's (2019) research into writing events with children from two to five years old, showed that both empty–handed gestures (without objects) and object gestures (holding an object) were significant modes of communication for preschoolers as well as the adults who were supporting them. This was most significant with the youngest children:

> As children pointed to the page with a pen in hand, they inscribed their gestures on the page, creating graphic arrays that indicated the target of joint attention. Adults foregrounded and reframed the child's inscribed gestures as emergent forms of writing, offering timely responses that provided opportunities to learn social expectations for writing processes, messages, and purposes. (Rowe, 2019, p. 13)

In Rowe's study, the adults' recognition and support of young children's gestures supported their early written language by establishing joint attention: 'meaning making was accomplished through the back-and-forth dance of hands as with the exchange of words' (2019, p. 31).

Speech, therefore, has an important role in supporting writing as a shared gesture. There is a well-established argument that talk is an essential ingredient in the creation of writing. Talk supports children's writing generation by giving them a way of rehearsing their writing ideas (Cremin and Myhill, 2012), enabling them to make decisions, and explore creative possibilities in response to the ideas of others. As children talk through their composition with others, the notion of writing as a socially meaningful communication, a dialogue between the writer and the 'reader', becomes explicit. This is why 'say it, write it' activities with children help to foster their writing production, as well as the metacognition needed to help them to recognise and reflect on how they can improve what they are doing (Fisher et al., 2010).

Reflection

Do you notice children talking through their writing ideas? Why do you think children might need to do this?

Emergent writing

The child viewed as an emerging writer is based on a developmental model of learning (Clay, 1975; Mayer, 2007). Emergent writing practices acknowledge the intentions of children in early mark-making as a communicative act (as discussed previously). This approach maps these creative experimentations with marks to norms of development, from the unconventional to the conventional (Clay, 1975). Teale and Sulzby, in their influential text *Emergent Literacy: Writing and Reading* (1994), argued that children develop writing as part of a linear process from birth with recognisable fixed stages that children pass through.

One of the most significant areas of a child's emergent writing is their name writing. Our experience has shown that young children really enjoy repeatedly writing their initial or whole name in many different ways. Name writing is an important predictor of children's future writing skills as it demonstrates that children have knowledge of the procedures of writing (letter shape formation, print concepts and spelling) (Puranik and Lonigan, 2012). By writing their name, children also know that writing has important functions, one of which is to identify yourself to others.

Although children can pass through developmental stages at different ages and in a variety of ways, emergent writing is 'forward looking', entailing an end stage when children become literate in the conventional sense. Emergent theories position children in relation to adult competences and, therefore, there is a risk that a deficit model of the child who is 'not yet literate' could be adopted as a result. There is also a focus on conventional or recognised 'standard' writing in this approach that does not question the cultural assumptions that surround standardisation, or consider how writing might be experienced by different children in diverse ways. Across the globe, writing is increasingly understood through a variety of graphical and textual forms. Children encounter writing in their day-to-day lives on screens, street signs, packaging as well as on the page and, therefore, they have knowledge of the range of functions, compositional features and procedures that writing has in the society they live in. It is important that this knowledge of writing is integrated into young children's literacy practices in early years settings.

Multiliteracies – writing as design

Thinking of young children's writing in terms of 'multiliteracies' has been extremely useful in recognising the diversity of voices and identities that exist within literacy practices at home, as well as in early educational settings (Pahl and Rowsell, 2005). A multiliteracy approach rejects a conformist or standard approach to texts arguing that this is very limiting when we consider the expansion and variety of communication modes and tools for meaning making that are on offer. If literacy is viewed by practitioners and teachers as multiple means of communication, then the cultural and linguistic diversity of our global communities can be represented, as well as the new technologies that are increasingly connecting these different communities together (New London Group, 1996).

As writers, children need to understand how conventional forms of writing are used alongside other forms of writing involving graphics and visual signs. Children should be aware of how these texts are multimodally produced so that they are able to produce them themselves through a process of redesign (Kress, 2000, 2003; Kress and Van Leeuwen, 2006). The idea of the child writer as a designer does not constrain, the child's abilities and literacy knowledge. Children can apply their knowledge of writing design (how text, graphics and space come together) into their own creations, elevating their abilities as communicators. Think again about how Charlie in the vignette at the beginning of this chapter had chosen to organise and design his marks and writing on the page as a way of listing the deliveries. He was transforming the writing knowledge he has into his redesign. The play he is engaging in is enabling this process.

How play supports children to compose written texts is explored further in the case study below. This case study focuses on how playfulness as something spontaneous – free from structure and manifesting joy and humour (Lieberman, 1977) – enables meaningful mark-making and writing. It incorporates many of the ideas presented in the chapter into real teaching scenarios.

Case Study

The Playful Writing Project

This year-long research project was carried out with six reception class teachers. It set out to explore how the ideas of play proposed by Froebel (as outlined in Chapter 1) could support children's engagement with mark-making, drawing and writing. It also intended to build teacher engagement in research, providing them with opportunities to develop their knowledge of early literacy and abilities in investigating their own practice. The teachers gathered data from their classrooms: observations, photographs, videos and reflective notes of children playing, mark-making and writing. They met together with the researcher monthly to discuss what they had noticed.

The teachers recognised that **the role of the adult** was very important in how playful writing was facilitated. The teachers agreed that the children needed 'time to get on and formulate ideas, to be left to it'. However, they recognised that they had an important part to play in spotting children's personal interests and supporting them in moving from individual playful activity to more collective play. They spoke of the ways in which they modelled different kinds of writing with children and demonstrated their own writing interests with children. One teacher described what they did with children in their classroom as 'seed planting', correlating with Froebelian notions of the adult as nurturer; another spoke of the sensitivity she needed to 'know when to skip in or out' of children's play. Another teacher felt that adults should protect children's rights to be free from judgements about their writing as this may affect the child's happiness and, therefore, motivation to write. They talked of a sense of 'wonder' in what children were doing. The teachers recognised that what children were writing and drawing in their play was not only socially and developmentally functional, but was also an emotionally positive experience for both adults and children.

The evidence collected showed that writing as part of the children's play took a multimodal form of communication that adopted other modes in the process of its composition. Talking, drawing and movement were integral features of how writing within play occurred, with many of the children's writing artefacts being made up of a mixture of mark-making, drawing, symbols and signs, that were shaped by the children's conversations, actions and the geographical spaces they moved through. Drawing as part of writing was viewed by the teachers as a crucial way in which children could 'share their worlds' with others in the learning environment.

From their reflective observations the teachers agreed that young children's playful writing activity had three features:

1. Social function,
2. Spontaneity and movement, and
3. Materiality.

(Continued)

1. The social function of playful writing

A good example of playful writing having social function was demonstrated by one of the teachers in her presentation of photographs and annotated observations of children playing a game of jumping over large blocks. This game, initially started by a few children, spiralled into a complex social event. At the beginning of the game, one child decided that it would be a good idea to keep a score of the players' jumps on the whiteboard with a series of ticks, this action led to other children joining in and keeping their own score cards, writing down ticks on old receipt rolls. This in turn led to the jumpers reading the scores to check that they were accurate, supporting purposeful reading as well as writing. Another child joined in the play and began to score using ones and zeros, and then one of the other scorers took this representative action one step further by writing down the names of who was in or out.

The teacher reflected on this playful mark-making and writing as having an important social function for the playing children: it extended the opportunities to play together. The children who participated were aware of what the writing was for and why it was important that they carried it out. The seriousness of the children's endeavour was also significant. The writing had to be accurate, checked and accountable to the experience of the group; the mark-making here had rules related to its social function, as all writing does, but also the writing was used to extend the play and increase the players' participation, the play grew in complexity and challenge both for the 'jumpers' and the 'scribers' as it continued. The integration of writing as social representation, as a functional tool, helped to develop the play, and the play helped to develop the writing: a symbiotic relationship.

Another example was when a group of children using chalks outside to draw lines on the playground to represent roads decided that they also needed signs to tell others in the class how to navigate the road, when to stop, and how to stay safe as road users. The writing and drawing together symbolised important communicative aspects of the play which encouraged children to engage with it as a collaborative event.

By adopting symbols (letters, shapes, numbers) within their play, the children's encounters became more socially adaptive to the needs of the group, more responsive to each other as players, more creative in finding ways to expand the play for everyone, and as a result, the play continued for longer periods of time.

2. Spontaneity and movement in playful writing

Children engaged in playful writing sometimes slowly (for enjoyment purposes) but often hurriedly, keen to get their ideas down. They moved

(Continued)

their play and writing from inside the classroom to outside, or from one area to another, and as they did this the function of the children's writing would change. As a result, the meanings the writing contained would alter, for example, a secret message was changed to become a map when the writing was moved outdoors. The children were revisiting their writing and redesigning it to make it more useful for another play experience – a process of semiotic redesign (Kress and Van Leeuwen, 2006). This 'recycling' of writing often involved movement – a repositioning in different spaces with different materials – and corresponds with Wohlwend's research where she noted that, 'Children engage in movement through time and space as they play. It is a dimension in which children are able to transform modes and transcend the expectations within school literacy discourse' (2008, p. 133).

3. Playful writing as materiality

The children actively sought out different resources and different spaces, both inside and out, in sometimes ingenious ways. However, the self-initiated and imaginative choices the children demonstrated in the materials they decided to use was also bounded by what was available. The ability to be playful as a writer was dependent on resources which may, or may not, lend themselves to being afforded multiple uses. Materials needed to provide something for the children, the items they used needed to 'say' something to them in the moment of their play.

The teachers were able to identify activities where materials acted upon children's thinking as writers; for example, in the space station role-play area the pencils were covered in silver foil and this encouraged the children to write as the pencils had acquired a different meaning through their material changes – they had become space pens, to write about space adventures. It is possible to infer that playful writing is materially inspired and that what is commonly referred to as 'the non-human' (Barad, 2007) is an essential element that gives rise to other aspects of playful writing. Children's material intra-actions are an essential part of this type of play. For playful writing to be able to have social function and be spontaneous children need to have the opportunity to be influenced by the potential of a diverse range of materials.

Finally

The close observation of children's writing that the teachers carried out during the year of the project increased their pedagogical knowledge so that they could plan, observe and interpret the meanings in children's mark-making, drawing and writing more effectively. This demonstrates the importance of observing children's play, or valuing it by noticing carefully what is happening. The teachers valued 'being in the moment'

(Continued)

with the children when they were writing and playing, although they also acknowledged the difficulties of not having enough time to play. They agreed that it was important to find the balance between making too many suggestions that challenge and support children's learning, and not disrupting play processes, or 'getting in the way of something spontaneous'. One teacher stated, 'It's all about the process, not the outcome, it's about finding the meanings for the child that are there'.

Froebel's ideas of the 'unity' of play (1887) can help us to understand how this works. The child's embodied mark-making actions, the effect the materials had on them, their thinking processes as they symbolised their ideas, as well as their developing social self in sharing this experience with others, were all present in these playful writing activities.

To find out more about this project, read Smith, K. and Jackson, K. (2018) Learning to be a writer: Why play really matters. *Early Years Educator*, 20 (4), 28–30.

Reflective questions

Have you observed children generating writing by engaging in these three playful features? What do you think educators should do to expand children's playful writing?

Practice ideas

Here are some practical ideas to support children's mark-making and writing that resulted from the Playful Writing Project.

- Create a resource area from which children can 'self-serve'. Include notepads, pencils, scissors, tape, crayons, whiteboards, chalk, letter magnets, clipboards, sticky notes, envelopes, post cards, rolls of paper, paper of different sizes and colours, and more.
- Collect old wallpapers. Use the backs of these to cover low areas of walls so that children can freely and spontaneously 'graffiti' on them. Children are thrilled when they know they can write on the walls!
- Sticky notes. These are quick and easy to use, fit in hands and pockets, and can be stuck in different places. An extension of this could be to have a message area where children and adults can leave messages for one another.
- UV pens. As they are 'invisible' they can be used anywhere. Use a UV torch to reveal the children's messages.
- 'On the go' box. Fill a carry box with a variety of writing equipment. This makes resources mobile and available for children to take with them as their play moves. Children's zip-up lunch bags also work well for these too.

— In summary —

- Mark-making, drawing and writing is symbolic, representing children's thoughts, experience and relationship to others.
- Writing is an embodied engagement with the material world. Children place great value on mark-making and writing objects their writing is extended as they move through different environments.
- Key features of play allow young children to produce diverse multimodal texts that serve a social function and encourage imagination and re-design.

Having read the chapter, here are some **discussion questions** to help you plan for young children's playful writing and mark-making.

1. What open-ended questions could you ask young children about their writing to help them to talk about their text-making process?

2. How could you foster children's multimodal authorship in early years settings and school classrooms? What ways could you 'publish' children's work for parents, carers and other children to read?

Further recommended reading

DCSF (2008) *Mark making Matters: Young Children Making Meaning in All Areas of Learning and Development.* London: DCSF [online]: www.foundationyears.org.uk/wp-content/uploads/2011/10/Mark_Marking_Matters.pdf [accessed 20/04/20]

Although this publication is linked to defunct government strategies, it is a really excellent resource that many early years practitioners still turn to. It contains some lovely examples of children's text making linked to the key principles of the EYFS and a good range of references to explore even further.

Hall, N. and Robinson, A. (2003) *Exploring Writing and Play in the Early Years* (2nd ed.). London: David Fulton.

Although this book may have been published a while ago and the references to policy are outdated, its central explanation of how play helps children to compose writing is really valuable.

5

SHARING STORIES: READING AND PLAYING TOGETHER

This chapter will

- help you to understand how playful activities support young children in learning to read;
- highlight the importance of regular family book sharing in the home;
- introduce you to different approaches to teaching reading, including Systematic Synthetic Phonics (SSP);
- encourage you to develop your own pedagogical choices in supporting young children's reading.

Reading is often viewed as an exercise in decoding written text. But to read is not only to crack the code of sounds and letters but also to make meaning of the words and phrases that the author has expressed. In this chapter, we will explore how learning to read can be enhanced through the interactive and intra-active qualities of play. We have already argued that play is a socially, culturally and materially rich 'space' that expands children's curiosity and imagination, one that engages them in deeper understandings of the world and relationships within it. These ideas can be extended to how children begin to read texts in print as well as on screen. Play spaces can extend children's understandings of the meanings ready to be explored and allow signs and texts to be 'played with'. Different types of print, both on the page and online, offer children opportunities to discover more about their immediate and wider world, and build connections with others and the wider community. To begin, let's consider how Sairah is building connections with others and with a printed text in the following vignette.

┤Vignette├───────────────────────────────

Reciprocal early reading encounters

Baby Sairah is 11 months old. She looks forward to the time after her bath when she sits on her father's lap for storytime. She eagerly selects her favourite book and her dad lifts her onto his lap to read the story. Sairah enjoys this special time with Dad. She enjoys snuggling into his chest as he opens the book. She smiles with anticipation of the story she knows so well. The book contains different animals behind flaps and as Sairah's dad reads the story, he encourages his daughter to make the corresponding animal noises. She enjoys imitating the animal sounds, her voice getting louder and louder. Her dad reciprocates her heightened playful mood. He pauses before lifting the next flap in the book. Sairah knows the book so well that she is able to make the animal noise without prompting. Her father praises her ability encouraging her to join in with reading the words on the next page of the book. She is able to repeat the rhythm of the story of the next page and cries out with delight as she lifts the flap independently and the next animal is revealed. When the story ends, Sairah looks to her dad and points to the book, wanting him to read it again, and so the reading interaction and intra-action between them and the book continues.

The beginnings of reading as social practice

If thinking originates from situated social interaction (Vygotsky, 1978), then the process of thinking needed to be a reader (the meaning that is made from the text) is also founded upon the social exchange between people and things in everyday life. To illustrate, moments after birth babies attempt to 'read' their mother's faces – they are trying to work out what the face they are looking at represents and importantly who they are in relation to what they are 'reading'. Through this process they are able to create meaningful relationships in response to who or what they are 'reading'. As very young children begin to explore their world beyond their primary carer they attempt to read a range of texts in a similar way by working out what 'signs' mean, from the graphics on the back of cereal packets, to emojis they see on phone screens, to the symbols on a remote control. Keen to find out how this information can help them understand their world and their place in it, reading for a young child is a necessary part of their day-to-day social, cultural and material existence.

From our experience as teachers and parents, children become literate as they derive meaning from print and understand the functions of language as a socially active process (Street, 2013). Reading text for young children necessitates their interaction with, and connection to, other people and materials. Young children are not passive in this process; they are actively reading to make sense of the print communications that they see around them, whether it is the adverts on the bus, menus in cafés, YouTube clips, magazines, text messages, or books, etc. To be a reader requires not only an understanding of how thoughts and words can be symbolised but also is a means to participate as a citizen of the world.

Taking this socio-cultural material perspective to reading helps us to recognise the multiple ways in which young children engage with reading materials in their day-to-day lives with their families, friends and communities. It also underlines how reading is inextricably linked to our social and material practices that change over time. How, where and with what we read – the technologies of reading – will be leading these transformations, and these changes should be represented in our educational settings to make reading meaningful.

Families reading together

Literacy learning begins at home and a wealth of research shows the importance of family book sharing for supporting children's literacy development (Luo and Tamis-LeMonda, 2019; Canfield et al., 2020). Significantly, young children's attainment in reading is predicated not on parents teaching children specific reading skills to achieve results, but on reading for pleasure (Schiefele et al., 2012). Family life is an enriched space for shared meaning making often driven by a sense of fun and enjoyment, making early reading encounters a positive and rewarding experience.

Taking pleasure in reading is at the forefront of the UK's Bookstart programme (BookTrust, n.d.). Bookstart gives babies and preschool age children free book packs via health visitors, library services and early years settings during their first year and then again when they are 3 and 4 years old. When questioned in evaluations of the programme, parents state that the book gifting, as well as the additional accompanying parental guidance has increased their book sharing time with their child and become the most popular way for them to enjoy being together. Book sharing is a way in which families are able to become socially and emotionally engaged together (Venn, 2014). Bookstart recommends that this is a daily event, or a family habit. The regularity of reading at home with children, particularly with children under three, not only helps to build family relationships but also increases children's understanding of language use and develops their vocabulary (Saracho, 2017).

Another literacy intervention programme that targeted parents, Early Words Together (National Literacy Trust, n.d.), that ran from 2013–15 with peer volunteers in 13 local authorities, aimed to improve the home learning environment of children aged two to five. The programme encouraged parents to extend and engage their children's communication, language and literacy through play, engagement and attachment. This resulted in significant improvements in the amount of parent–child talk, children's comprehension of spoken language, and their engagement with songs and rhymes (Wood et al., 2015). The programme also demonstrated positive outcomes with families who were often experiencing social or economic disadvantage, helping these children to increase their vocabulary, attention to, and enjoyment of reading.

Importantly, these programmes show parents how reading can be integrated into the broader play activities that occur in everyday family life. According to Kenney (2016), book sharing provides parents with a 'way into' play, giving them ideas, vocabulary and questions to ask their children, resulting in greater parental confidence in knowing how to play with their children. She recommends that parents incorporate props and re-enactments, include siblings and friends, and encourage physical movement in their book sharing activities with children (Kenney, 2016).

Encouraging all parents and carers, whatever their background, to share books at home with their children sends a message about the importance of reading with children. Enjoying the tactile intra-active qualities of books is a sensory experience for both carer and child. However, there are practical barriers for parents and carers to overcome in finding time and energy for reading with their children. Significantly, fathers are less likely to read with their children than mothers due to working hours (Fatherhood Institute, 2010), and so educators of young children need to work with families to provide the support necessary to overcome some of these structural barriers which may lead to disadvantage.

Reflection

What books have you read yourself that include flaps, sliding and tactile parts, squeakers, pictures and other features that could be used to provide parents with a 'way into play'? How might you initiate families' engagement in play-based book sharing?

Visual literacy and picture books

Visual literacy is a linguistic tool that recognises that we are communicating with each other and exchanging ideas increasingly based on visual images, particularly in the digital world. Effective communication, therefore, is becoming more reliant on visual literacies. To become effective readers, young children need to be able to decipher and understand the meanings of not only words, but also other modes of textual communication, e.g. colour, design on a page, diagrams, images (both still and moving). Picture books help them to do this by providing them with multimodal narratives that encourage them to make meaning of the story through the amalgam of writing and pictures on the page. There is a synergy between these modes of communication that supports children's understanding of both the meanings of the words and the story that is being told. The interplay of words and images also open up new spaces or gaps for the child to fill in with their own playful imagination (Arizpe, 2014). Some illustrators of picture books, for example Lauren Child and Lynne Chapman, are very clever in maximising visual signs and blurring the boundaries between the writing and illustrations, using typography that draws children's attention to letters and numbers, and stimulating colour and design to engage the young reader to find further meaning in the story that is being told.

Baird et al. (2015) in their research with twenty-four seven- and eight-year-olds, found that children often concentrated on small elements in a picture as a way of making sense of the whole text. This was reinforced by the dialogue overheard between the children that often focused on the small details of images from which they made meaning together. The children used their personal experiences to help them understand the ideas within the story and created their own elaborations of the narrative, otherwise known as 'fictionality' (Nikolajeva and Scott, 2006). These interactions with picture books demonstrated the children's developing understanding of how reading works. They were able to enter the world of the text and create real and imaginative connections to it, as well as problem solve the finer details, all elements necessary in being a successful reader.

The connections between the child and the book, particularly the child's sense of themselves within the text, has been explored by Evans (2012) in a study with three-year-olds. Evans argues that when children have picture books shared with them, they are able to identify a sense of self that is mirrored in the text; recognising themselves in the storybook narratives which then interestingly inform their choice of favourite books. The children in Evans' study were able to express their ideas about books in differing modes (e.g. drawing and speech) demonstrating the interplay between reading and authoring, where children bring their own selves and their imagination, to transform the text into something of their own.

The following case study illustrates how Betty encourages three-year-old Lewis to gradually participate in sharing stories with others.

Case Study

Sharing Stories

Three-year-old Lewis has happily settled into his preschool. It has been observed by his preschool teacher, Betty, that he is keen to sit in the book corner, on the carpet and look through the picture books for extended periods of time. When other children approach, he closes the book guardedly in case they try to take it away. He appears to enjoy his own company, but Betty is concerned that he does not seem willing to share his books with others. At home time, Betty decides to ask his mother whether he enjoys

(Continued)

sharing stories at home and discovers that he 'prefers to watch a video before bedtime rather than reading stories'.

Betty begins to wonder whether his possession over the books in the book corner is the result of a lack of opportunities to share and to enjoy stories with others. Over the next few weeks, Betty creates opportunities for more shared story times in small groups and notices that over time, Lewis becomes more confident joining in with shared stories. He particularly likes the stories that have colourful illustrations with animated characters. She notices that he enjoys a series of books where vehicles have characters and can talk – he can see this as he understands that the vehicles have speech bubbles indicating what they are saying.

Betty appreciates the importance of supporting children to engage in meaning-making activities through relating stories to objects. She deliberately sets up opportunities for Lewis to engage in small world role play with the mini vehicles that they have in the setting. She plays alongside Lewis, making vehicle noises and uses more directed technical language as she re-enacts the stories that she had shared during story time. To her delight, she discovers that Lewis begins to reciprocate and play with her, making suggestions about what happens next. Over time, he requests her company and as he becomes more confident in his ability to lead this play, she notices that he is more assertive in the shared reading sessions. He is willing to talk about the feelings of the characters in the story and suggest reasons for their behaviour. Betty is delighted that he is more confident to use language and technical words such as 'construction' and 'fire hose' to engage in exploring the meaning behind the characters' actions in the stories. She is pleased that Lewis is able to draw on his experiences of play to join in with the shared stories with others in his group and even more delighted that he asks to take the books home to share with his family.

Reflective questions

How does Betty help Lewis to begin to share his stories? How does she develop this further?

What does Betty notice about Lewis' storytelling language and how could this be further supported?

Reading debates

The reading strategies that schools adopt influence the activities that early years settings do in helping children to get 'ready for school'. Preparing children for what is to come is understandable; however, based on what we know about how young children learn, implementing formal reading activities that are incongruent with play sometimes many months and years before children are due to start school, is problematic. It is important that practitioners make thoughtful decisions about how early reading is planned within early years settings that resist reductive school readiness agendas and instead encourage children's natural desire to read as well as their active participation in reading communities.

The teaching of reading has been the subject of significate debate over the last 50 years which has at times led to an over-simplified understanding of the reading process. On one side of the debate is the 'whole language' approach which draws on John Dewey's ideas about learning as child-centred discovery, and focuses specifically on reading as a process of meaning making (Smith, 1992; Goodman, 2005). This approach advocates using 'real' books that children are able to select themselves and encourages children to rely on a range of cues, or ways of making sense of the text (e.g. word order, sentence structure, grapho-phoneme correspondence). Advocates of this approach argue that children learn how the smaller parts of language work by focusing on how they all come together as a 'whole'. Positioned as being on the other side of the reading debate is the 'decoding' approach which introduces text to children primarily as individual components or parts that can be built up bit by bit in order of complexity. This is a bottom-up approach based on learning skills that can be applied to decode the text (e.g. letter–sound relationships, and letter patterns). This approach is evident in explicit, systematic phonics instruction – see the section on Systematic Synthetic Phonics (SSP) later on in the chapter.

Whatever reading approach or combination of approaches that educators adopt, our experience of working with young children tells us not to lose sight of the fact that reading is about making meaning, a process where the child needs to recognise themselves within the text and understand the lives of others, as well as create imagined possibilities. Making sense of the world and making sense of text as a reader, happens through social interaction with other people – both the author as the writer of the text, as well as the carer, practitioner or peer who the child is reading with. To enhance this process, Zevenbergen and Whitehurst (2003) recommend 'Dialogic Reading' with shared picture books, where the adult engages the child with 'what' questions as well as other open-ended questioning. The adult also repeats and expands what the child says, praises and encourages them, and follows their interests. Done in a fun way Zevenbergen and Whitehurst state that dialogical reading leads to greater gains as it scaffolds narrative skills, supports the understanding of syntax (word order) and leads to children's greater use of vocabulary.

Alongside the social interaction between the adult and the child, intra-action between the child and the material text also occurs as part of reading, for example, when children turn the pages of a book or touch a screen. Young children need to be encouraged to be active readers by playing with the materiality of texts; engaging with their sensorial qualities to gain further meanings and understandings from the reading process.

Importantly, young children bring prior knowledge to their reading encounter and will be creating new thoughts and feelings associated with reading. Children can use their prior experience as language users together with their imagination to predict, self-correct, discuss and be expressive, as well as decipher the meaning of letters, words and sentences. In this way, reading for young children is a process of problem solving, of applying what they know already about different word meanings and sentence construction, what visual images represent, as well as how different graphical shapes are linked to different phonemes (letter sounds).

Rhymes, patterns and phonological awareness

One of the most famous children's writers who uses rhyme and pattern is Dr Seuss. It is fascinating to consider why the books he wrote seventy years ago are still so popular with younger and older readers alike, despite recent criticisms in the United States of the lack of diversity and cultural stereo-typing in some of his stories. His quirky illustrations and often subversive characters are great fun, but more enduring is the rhyme and rhythm of the language that pull together the humour and adventure within the books; language that is very enjoyable to read out loud. Dr Seuss's books, like other successful child authors, for example, Michael Rosen (*Little Rabbit Foo Foo*), Julia Donaldson (*The Gruffalo*), and Janet and Allan Ahlberg (*Each Peach, Pear Plum*) use repetitive patterns, alliteration and rhymes to make the language 'sing' to children and encourage them to join in with the text. The words in the book are easily remembered and help children predict what is coming as well as giving movement to the story that carries the child along.

Margaret Mooney's research (1990) noted that children are more able to move on to reading by themselves, not only if they are read to regularly using books with strong picture/text relationships, but also if the books that are being shared have patterned and predictable language. Ushi Goswami's neuroscientific research (2010) on speech development and early reading helps to further explain the importance of this patterning or the 'musicality' of language in books as a reading aid, by showing that our neural oscillators are fired in response to the rhythms in language. These rhythmic patterns are part of speech as well as other modes of communication, e.g. dance and clapping games. They form the sound structures of language, otherwise known as phonology. Children's phonological awareness is raised through the emphasis on the rhythms of words and syllables, and the repeated patterns in songs and stories. This language play helps the reader to tune into the language within the text and promotes phonology as a foundation for literacy.

Neaum (2017) also draws our attention to the importance of other types of language play as a regular feature of these types of text – the puns, jokes, double-meanings and the unorthodox use of words. These features enable children to focus on the structure of language and the importance of grammar. This also supports semantic development, as playing with words – making up nonsensical words and phrases – focuses children's attention on how to read to find meaning.

Playfully patterned rhyme focuses children's attention on the sounds, pronunciation and fluency of language represented in text, a step towards being able to recognise grapheme–phoneme correspondences. This type of language play helps children to develop their auditory skills by tuning into the properties of sounds and eventually to develop their phonemic awareness where they can hear, identify and manipulate different oral sounds. It is important that children are proficient at this before being explicitly taught phonics otherwise they may struggle to distinguish how different sounds represent different symbols, or be able to say the sounds that the symbols represent. Effective approaches to phonics advocate activities that do this as a first phase, emphasising the need to support young children to hear, attend and respond to sounds so they can build phonological awareness and sensitivity before moving towards more formal instruction.

The following case study illustrates how Kwame, a reception teacher, has used his observations of the space-themed play that his children were enjoying to create new opportunities for them to experience rhyme and alliteration.

Case Study

Supporting Children's Meaning Making

Kwame is a reception teacher. Before the beginning of term, he spent a lot of time making his reading corner attractive and inviting. It appears to have paid off and he has noticed that there are a small group of children in his class who particularly enjoy reading the 'Amazing Machines' series (Mitton, 2017). Kwame chose these books because of their rhyming appeal and brightly coloured pictures that illustrate the technical language in the text. He notices that lately, the children in the group have chosen to look through the *Roaring Rockets* book several times and then have attempted to make their own rockets in the construction corner. Kwame decides to capture their enthusiasm for space travel and plans to develop their knowledge and understanding of space. He reads the book to them and pauses as he reads to give the children an opportunity to say the rhyming words before checking their understanding of these.

The children don't need much encouragement to help him to construct a space station in the role-play area. They manage to make a space rocket out of some old crates and large pieces of thin card, a mission control centre with dials and gadgets drawn on pieces of cardboard and a cabin for the crew to sit in when they take charge of the rocket. The children play enthusiastically in this area and, as they play, Kwame observes them discussing the controls and their purposes.

(Continued)

Kwame decides to capture this opportunity to make a book with them to develop their phonological awareness. He knows that writing for a purpose is key in motivating young children to make meaning from text and sets about suggesting that they make a large book together so that the 'engineers' will be able to tell everyone what the gadgets and machinery are for. He encourages them to make alliterative suggestions to describe the machines. Together they want to write 'the rusty, rattling, rocket with the weeny, whistling, widget that shimmers and shines'. Kwame encourages the children to have a go at writing the words underneath their pictures and repeat the alliterative words with emphasis upon each phoneme as they read their writing.

Reflective questions

How does Kwame arrange his environment to further support children's meaning making through the texts that they read?

What might motivate children to engage in co-creating texts? What purposes might enthuse them?

Systematic synthetic phonics (SSP)

Synthetic phonics is a decoding strategy where a child is supported to read, for example 'cat', by being taught that the letter 'c' represents the /c/ sound, the letter 'a' the /a/ sound, the letter 't' the /t/ sound, and that to make the word they need to blend (synthesise) the sounds together. A systematic approach to this is to teach grapheme–phoneme (letter–sound) correspondences in a planned and sequential order, starting with the simple most frequent grapheme–phonemes and progressing to the less common, as well as clusters of graphemes that represent phonemes (digraphs). Since 2010, the government has set out requirements for schools and teacher training providers to adopt Systematic Synthetic Phonics (SSP) as the main method for teaching reading in the UK, stressing the need to organise the teaching of this into discrete short daily sessions designed to progress from simple elements to the more complex aspects of phonic knowledge, skills and understanding. The government has recommended specific programmes, or 'products' that schools can purchase, in order to make sure they are working within this approach. This has raised concerns about how the teaching of reading has now become a specifically marketised area of education that commercial interests are able to influence.

The SSP approach was influenced by Jim Rose's review of reading (Rose, 2005) that sought to identify the best practices in supporting early reading in UK schools. The report critiqued the then common approach to reading in schools, commonly known as the 'Searchlight System'. This approach had been influenced by Marie Clay's cueing system model (1985), where children 'searched' for sources of knowledge to help illuminate the text they were reading: phonic, grammatical, word recognition and contextual. By drawing on psychological perspectives, Rose argued that for effective teaching it was important to distinguish between two specific processes or elements in learning to read: word recognition and language comprehension. This he called the 'Simple View of Reading'. Rose argued that individual word meanings are identified from phonological input and, therefore, explicit phonic teaching enabled word recognition.

The report drew on research from a series of studies in Clackmannanshire, Scotland (Johnston and Watson, 2005) where 300 children in their first year of school were divided into three groups, each learning with a different type of phonics method. At the end of a 16-week period, the synthetic phonics taught group were reading words around seven months ahead of the other two groups and were eight to nine months ahead in spelling. The performance of the synthetic phonics group continued in measurements nine months later, even when the other groups were also being taught in the same way, showing the importance of beginning and maintaining a systematic approach. From this evidence, the Rose Report concluded that, 'synthetic phonics ... offers the vast majority of beginners the best route to becoming skilled readers' (Rose, 2005, p. 19).

Concerns and disputes surrounding SSP approaches

There have been criticisms of the research design of the Clackmannanshire studies, particularly the lack of rigour in how the groups were compared and the empirical evidence that can be drawn from the studies as a result (Wyse and Goswami, 2008). Margaret Clark (2014) has also questioned missing elements from the Rose Report around the teaching of SSP approaches; for example, how they support children who are already competent and fluent readers when they begin instruction, or those who have specific language difficulties. To add to this, Clark (2013) raises concerns about the assessment practices that surround SSP approaches, particularly the validity of the current Year 1 phonics check and how it is influencing a 'teaching to the test' approach. Recent analysis of other studies has also concluded that no one method of teaching phonics appears to be superior to any other (Torgerson et al., 2019). This has led to questions about why one approach, based on disputed evidence, has been so influential. Although phonics has historically been integrated into most reading strategies, there is still an ongoing debate about whether one method of teaching phonics is better than others.

Importantly, in reviewing best practice the Rose Report stated that it was active, multi-sensory phonics practice that was most effective (2005, p. 3), thus recognising the importance of children's agency, movement and sensorial experience in learning phonics. Even though Rose distinguishes between word recognition and comprehension of the text, he also advocated a programme of phonic work that should be securely embedded within a broad and language-rich curriculum, one that demonstrates discussion and comprehension (2005, p. 16). Rose, therefore, emphasises the need for young children to make connections between phonics skills and other areas of language and communication, particularly talk, in order for them to fully understand how they function. When Rose advocated the 'Simple View of Reading', SSP was considered to be taught alongside reading comprehension. When young children learn to read, they should they be mastering grapheme-phoneme correspondence as a way of making meaning of whole texts. In concluding this section, we agree with Wyse and Goswami (2008) in disputing the simplification of this process. Reading they state is 'one the most complex achievements' (p. 706) that young children are able to accomplish and, importantly, how well they achieve this will be affected by the socio-material resources available to them.

Reflection

What pedagogical approaches to reading would you advocate? How would you justify them to others?

Extending reading with real and digital materials

Book sharing with children in groups is a common feature of early years classrooms and research has shown the importance of involving props to extend the meaning gained from the text (Saracho, 2017). Book sharing is a useful stepping stone towards other play activities. Role play stimulated by book sharing, for example, is a way of re-enacting and extending the story, and supports children with reading comprehension, language skills and creativity (Moedt and Holmes, 2020). Studies have shown that children gain greater expressive vocabulary and extend their abilities in using receptive and expressive speech during adult-led play-based activities when this play is extended from book sharing activities (Touba et al., 2018). These positive effects on language and literacy are also seen when children are engaged in purposeful self-selected play based around the books that have been shared with them (Moedt and Holmes, 2020).

Story sacks were initially developed by Neil Griffiths (2001) to encourage reading at home and extend the child's understanding of the story and the meanings that it contains. A story sack is a large attractive cloth bag containing a well-written and illustrated children's picture book with supporting materials to stimulate reading activities in order to support both book sharing and the extension of further opportunities in developing language. The book's characters, props, setting and story are all represented in the artefacts contained in the sack – these could take the form of masks, puppets, dressing up items, language games, writing and drawing materials, and specific objects from the story used as 'hooks' on which children can hang their retelling (Whitehead, 2007, p. 78). Story sacks enhance the intra-active qualities of reading, as they are materially stimulating. They also draw on the type of narrative play outlined in the last chapter that intends to extend children's imagination and storytelling as authors themselves.

Much of our previous discussion about sharing picture books with children in playful ways, can also be extended to digital texts and e-readers. The following chapter will look in more detail about digital literacy; however, it is worth noting the importance of multimodal digital stories and how they are effective in supporting children's reading of stories. Wohlwend (2017) recommends that practitioners need to look beyond print-intensive reading/writing workshops with children in order to envision a more playful digital early childhood curriculum. She argues that as digital tools make up modern cultural communication, incorporating digital reading opportunities would enhance greater opportunities for children's participation as literacy users and makers within their play.

Flewitt et al. (2015) in their research on the use of iPads in a range of early years settings showed that young children's reading activities could be viewed as hybridised events as children moved between reading real books and digital devices. This hybridity helped to support the reading process; for example, when one child was able to transfer knowledge of word recognition from an iPad spelling game into the reading scheme books, enhancing his reading abilities. iPads, with their intuitive touchscreen qualities and portability, are hugely motivational for children as they offer engaging multimodal literacy experiences that support children to become enthused about reading for meaning. Research into the use of iPads with toddlers by Cekaite and Björk-Willén (2018) has also highlighted the importance of teachers and adults in mediating stories from the screen into real life for children. The preschool teachers in their study used the visual information on iPad screens as a launchpad to share the aesthetic pleasures of stories. Importantly, it was the sweeping gaze of the teacher across the children to solicit and sustain listening and to monitor the children's participation with the story, as well as their facial expressions and language that dramatised the story and held the children's attention.

Miller and Warschauer (2014) also suggest that e-reading may be particularly beneficial for younger children reading on their own without the support of parents due to scaffolding opportunities embedded in the text, for example, the text-to-speech tools (read aloud) facilities. They also add that font size manipulation, dictionaries, automatic page turning and animation hotspots are advantageous over traditional print sources in supporting young children's understanding and independence in reading.

Whatever the materials for reading, the supportive and sensitive interaction between the adult and child to bring books to life in playful ways is paramount. Together with this, the intra-active qualities that books (whether it be a traditional book or a digital device) offer in the form of visual, tactile and moveable features needs to be foregrounded in planning for rich and motivational early reading encounters.

┤Practice ideas├

Here are some practical ideas to support children's reading as part of their play:

- Have non-fiction books available and open on selected pages to entice children to relate the content to their play. For example, books about transport could be available next to the small world play resources such as trains, cars and people.
- Enable children to create and share digital books on interactive whiteboards and tablets if these are available.
- Staple together some different sized pieces of paper as 'books' for children to illustrate and write their own stories. Encourage the authors of these stories to read them at story time and take them home to share with their families.
- As you join in with children's play, capture their stories and turn them into books to share more widely with the setting and school community. There are some lovely examples here that detail children's stories created with their educators: https://helicopterstories.co.uk/
- Use your local library to source copies of 'big books'. These giant-sized books are perfect for sharing with a group of children, especially if you involve the children in turning the pages and pointing at the words with a pointer as you all read together.

┤In summary├

- Encouraging parents to share books with their children from birth is an important way to foster regular reading behaviour as well as positive family relationships.
- Book sharing with children helps younger children to extend their vocabulary, recognise the rhythms of language, and enhances their enjoyment of the reading process.
- Picture books encourage children to develop wider literacy awareness, including visual literacy.
- Practitioners should support children to develop their phonological awareness within play activities before they begin the formal teaching of phonics.
- Reading environments should include a range of quality books as well as digital reading devices that are easily accessible and used to enhance play.

Having read this chapter, here are some **discussion questions** to help you in planning young children's playful reading activity:

1. Think about where the books and texts are located in your setting. Are they available in different locations or just in the book corner? Could they be relocated? Do you share these with families and, if not, how possible might this be?

2. When and how do you share books? Have you fallen into a routine of having them at particular times of the day? Could you use stories to stimulate children's thinking at other times? For example, to stimulate a mathematical problem? Or to create books of their own?

Further recommended reading

Bower, V. (Ed.) (2014) *Developing Early Literacy: From Theory to Practice 0–8*. London: Sage.

This excellent edited book has chapters on all aspect of early literacy, including ones that focus on developing reading environments, rhythm and rhyme, and picture books.

Neaum, S. (2017) *What Comes Before Phonics?* London: Sage.

An engaging book that covers all aspects of early literacy and is really helpful in showing the relationship between phonological awareness, phonics and reading.

6

PLAYING DIGITALLY: MULTIMODAL DIGITAL LITERACIES

━ This chapter will ━

- support your understanding of how digital play can support young children's literacies;
- familiarise you with recent research on how different digital tools and applications (e.g. touchscreens, apps, e-books, etc.) support children's literacies;
- help you to reflect on how early years educators can integrate digital literacy practices into day-to-day literacy learning.

Young children are part of a changing digital world. The social and cultural practices that surround digital technologies provide increasing ways for young children to participate, to be agentive and creative with others. Digital technologies are an important part of every-day literacies; in order to be fully literate, children need to be dexterous readers and writers of both digital and non-digital texts (Neumann et al., 2017). Digital technologies can be viewed as mediational tools – young children are able to think with these tools to extend their narrative play and support specific reading and writing skills. They use these technologies as authors, creating digital content by merging videos, photos, writing and graphics, enabling them to connect and communicate across the world fostering connection with family and friends. As readers, they make meaning of multimodal digital texts containing text, audio, visual illustrations, animations and design.

Digital technologies are material things; their physical properties affect the possibilities for literacy play. As we will explore in this chapter, the malleability of digital materials can add to the richness of young children's literacy encounters. For example, technology is an increasingly portable thing, meaning that children can play with digital technologies in different spaces at different times and for different purposes. This adaptability encourages children to creatively blend digital technologies and non-digital materials together within their play. Examining how children use and adapt digital and traditional technologies in their play helps us to reveal how multiliteracy activity is generated (Kress, 2003), and amplifies the need to recognise these informal, yet vital, literacy play experiences.

This chapter will focus explicitly on young children's play with digital toys, games and applications as part of everyday literacy, looking at how these digital technologies are used collaboratively and fused with more traditional play materials and activities. Digital technologies include a vast range of constantly changing and emerging devices, so it isn't possible for us to examine all of these in this chapter; instead, we encourage you to make links as you read with other types of technology, and consider in your reflections how these might also support young children's literacies.

Digital debates and deliberations

Early years educators may be aware of the digital experiences that young children have outside of educational settings and even recognise the skills that children need in order to be digitally literate; however, debates within the early childhood sector about the influence that digital technologies have in young children's lives continue (Arnott et al., 2019). On the one hand, as we have done in our introduction, it can be argued that digital technology as a part of everyday global communication can enhance children's connection with the world and create potential for multimodal creative play. On the other, there are concerns about the extent to which playing with devices is problematic for a range of reasons: the addictive algorithms within the design of apps and games; the infiniteness and, therefore, unmanageable nature of the internet; and the potential risks of children having access to information and unknown people, as examples. There are also worries that if children are spending too much time using digital devices, sensory and physical play experiences could be neglected, as well as opportunities to build essential connections with the natural world.

The tensions surrounding the development of digital literacies are rooted in the value placed on play-based pedagogy and the potential (or not) within those pedagogical beliefs for digital technologies to be able to be integrated successfully into early years education to improve the quality of learning (Vidal-Hall et al., 2020). Adult educators have concerns themselves about their own over-reliance on screens, the addictive qualities of social media, and the sedentary lifestyle that digital screen use is creating. The fears we have about the exponential growth of digital technologies as part of children's lives are therefore situated alongside social worries, indicating that our troubling over digital pedagogy is representative of wider social anxieties about digital life. Combined with a notion that childhoods were simpler when technology was not so pervasive, it is unsurprising that some early years 'early childhood' practitioners are reluctant to encourage digital use. Furthermore, these deliberations are unhelpfully underpinned by contrasting ideas of young digital users themselves. As Marsh (2018, p. 55) writes,

> On the one hand, children are viewed as digital experts, navigating a range of technologies with intuitive expertise, and on the other they are positioned as the innocent victims of a globalised and highly commercialised technology industry, driven to zombified or aggressive cognitive states through an addictive use of various media.

Research has shown that practitioners' cultural beliefs and philosophies of learning – the underpinning image of the child as learner – appear to impact on how cautious or not practitioners are in integrating technology into their day-to-day practices. For example, educators in England are more sceptical than those in Norway of using touchscreen technologies with children under three (Fotakopoulou et al., 2020). A more positive stance towards technology in Norway may be as a result of a more digitalised society where practitioners are more confident digital users themselves, and where valuing children's skills and participation in using digital technologies in terms of their future citizenship is recognised.

It has also been noted that there are curricular-specific tensions that pit digital literacies against traditional literacy learning. For example, in England, the emphasis on children reaching certain standards in print literacy means that early years teachers have difficulties in positioning and rationalising digital technologies as a pedagogical tool. Early years teachers report that they feel pressure to find a balance between digital and print learning, or that one is in opposition to the other (Daniels et al., 2020). In Sweden, research similarly shows that preschool teachers' conceptualisations of digital media are limited to supporting specific curriculum competences or even viewed as a threat to notions of 'real' communication (Hernwall, 2016).

Considering the anxieties and pressures that may exist, it is important that educators have time and space to critically reflect on their own early childhood philosophies and how these relate to digital technologies, as well as recognising their own skills and competencies as digital players.

Reflection

How confident are you in supporting young children with their play-based digital literacy skills? Are there technologies that you feel more able to support children with? Or technologies that children might be able to support *you* with? What do you believe young children should be doing with technologies to support their learning?

Technology is an additional 'language' that children can use to express themselves and communicate meaning (Marsh et al., 2020), so beginning with understanding how digital technologies can enhance play (and vice versa) is a good way to explore how that expression and communication can be realised. Observing children in their play with digital technology shows us that digital literacy is not separate to other literacies – not an add on, or an alternative – but an integrated process of learning about how literacies can be used and explored to enhance meaning making.

Defining digital literacy

Although the term 'digital literacy' is used in many educational contexts, there are many ways to conceptualise its meaning, so it remains ambiguous (Daniels et al., 2020). Digital literacy refers to a wide range of activities, skills and abilities in using and adapting increasingly diverse technologies and environments. In this chapter, we are focusing on the relationship between digital literacy and play; however, it is important to note that digital literacy as globally significant to education is often framed as a way in which to develop digitally competent future citizens (Vuorikari et al., 2016; Marsh et al., 2020). Having considered the economic and rights-based argument for all children to become digitally literate, UNICEF have defined digital literacy as,

> the set of knowledge, skills, attitudes and values that enable children to confidently and autonomously play, learn, socialize, prepare for work and participate in civic action in digital environments. Children should be able to use and understand technology, to search for and manage information, communicate, collaborate, create and share content, build knowledge and solve problems safely, critically and ethically, in a way that is appropriate for their age, local language and local culture. (p. 32)

In writing this book we were particularly interested in how young children's literacies are generated and modified through, and with, digital technologies, and how play facilitates this. We recognise the importance for children's digital literacy play to prepare children for their future and to enable them to manage risk, and argue that in order to foster the skills necessary for access to civil society we focus on the young child as an active and creative digital user/player. This conceives the child as both a consumer of multimodal texts (a reader) and a producer of such texts (a writer) (Erstad and Gillen, 2019).

Highlighting children's right to be digitally literate means responding to the significant inequalities that exist in digital literacy opportunities within children's homes, where access to digital technologies is mixed, and family practices variable (Stephen et al., 2013; Chaudron et al., 2015). For example, poorer families are more likely to rely on free apps which lack creative potential and are crowded with advertisements (Marsh et al., 2015). A 'digital divide' therefore exists, meaning that children are affected by differences in infrastructure, class and cultural preferences leading to inequalities in accessing material resources (Marsh et al., 2020). The integration of digital technologies within day-to-day planning of play activities in early years settings and classrooms can perform a significant role in bridging this inequitable technological divide and enabling the growth of digital literacy within society.

Developing good quality digital play

There are an abundance of digital tools and applications that can be used to support young children's engagement in digital literacy practices; however, this presents early years educators with challenges in deciding how best to design and scaffold digital play, particularly how to identify the potential pedagogical benefits of each. Digital toys, applications and devices have varying degrees of quality and flexibility, so it is necessary that practitioners critically evaluate the effectiveness of digital tools in supporting children's diverse playful literacies. In making these critical decisions, a recognition of the qualities of digital play must be central.

Play has multiple theories and perspectives attached to it (see Chapter 1), so defining and recognising the value that digital play holds for young children and how it can be integrated into play pedagogy is multifaceted and therefore challenging (Edwards, 2018). There have been attempts nevertheless to understand how digital play might look in an early years setting, as well as provide frameworks for early years educators to use. For example, Edwards and Bird (2017) have developed a Digital Play Framework by drawing on Vygotskian ideas of language and play, arguing that without a basis for understanding how children learn to use technologies through play it is difficult for educators to observe and assess young children's technological learning. This assessment tool provides educators with 'indicators' of children's digital play. They explain that as children learn to use technologies as tool mediation (to think with), they move from epistemic play where the children are building knowledge of things (how things work and what they do), through to ludic play where they are drawing on their past experiences and including symbolic and fantasy elements (Hutt, 1979).

Young children also extend their knowledge of digital tools, not only through hands-on use, but through imaginative role play, where digital tools are 'present' in their play but generated using non-digital materials. The vignette below, showing the experiences of two children who are fascinated with the technology in their nursery that is designed to keep them safe, illustrates this type of analogue/digital play. There is something about the mystery surrounding a 'secret code' that draws them in and arouses their curiosity. You can see how their key worker notices this and gently introduces a way to enable them to engage in transporting their real-life experience into a form of role play. This enables them to express and communicate their knowledge of digital literacy, and transform what they know into a material object, a process that also incorporates other literacy skills (reading and writing skills).

Vignette

Merging digital and analogue literacies

Anna and Jack, aged four, are fascinated by the keypad that they had seen at their nursery. They have observed their educators using it to gain access to the storeroom. They are intrigued by the idea of pressing particular buttons in a particular order to release the lock and have tried to imitate this by drawing up a chair, standing on it and jabbing at the keys. Nancy, their key worker, smiles at them, with the intention of gently moving them away from the keypad she suggests that perhaps they should make their own. 'What could we use?' she asks them. 'How about this?' says Jack, as he grabs a piece of paper from the drawer. 'Good idea,' Anna responds, as she reaches across a nearby table to grab a felt-tip pen. Jack competently draws a grid to represent the keypad, before carrying it over to the existing keypad to make a note of the numbers. He carefully replicates the numbers in the same order on the paper. He shows great involvement in this task, looking carefully at each number, and then looking down at his paper to slowly and carefully, copy each of the numbers in the same position on his paper. While he is doing this, Anna draws around her hand on another piece of paper. Once she has done this, she takes it over to Jack, saying 'look, I've made a hand scanner. We can use this to stop the robbers getting in.' 'Yes,' agrees Jack. 'I know,' says Anna thoughtfully, 'we can stick this on the wall over there so that we can stop the robbers getting into our play.'

Digital play can expand our notions of play, as new types of play can be observed, and different play skills are learnt when children engage with digital media. Edwards (2013) for example has highlighted that young children's play has adjusted to the developmental demands of the digital context where children need to be more critically aware as consumers, more sophisticated in their problem-solving abilities, and more adaptive to new cultural knowledge. Marsh et al. (2016) have shown that not only can young children's digital play be 'placed' within established typographies of play it can also extend these typographies by introducing new ones. In their extensive study of children's digital play practices, they identified a new type – transgressive play, occurring for example where children use features of apps that were not part of their original design, transgressing the intentions of the manufacturers. Transgressive play they argue, is 'Play in which children contest, resist and/or transgress expected norms, rules and perceived restrictions in both digital and non-digital contexts' (Marsh et al., 2016, p. 250).

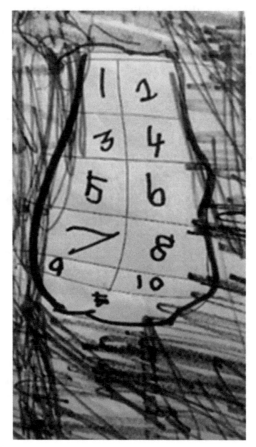

Figure 6.1   Jack's digital keypad

─ Reflection ─

How would you define digital literacy play? What aspects of play do you think link to children's use of digital technology? Have you observed children engaged in transgressive play?

Digital literacies within the home

Observing digital literacy play practices at home as well as within other non-formal learning environments, e.g. libraries and museums, is a good place to begin in understanding the potential that digital play has in supporting literacy. Marsh et al.'s (2015) research into children's use of apps at home involving 2,000 parents and carers of children under five years as well as six case studies families, found that the digital games and activities that fostered social interaction with parents and siblings were the ones that children were most keen to engage with. Technology was mentioned by parents as a means of developing shared cultural understandings; for families who spoke languages other than English, digital media offered a way of communicating their language and culture. Consequently, home was, for the majority of children in this study a rich site for technological experience that promoted social relationships and family culture.

Research has also shown how parent–child shared storytelling can be extended with iPad apps that enable the creation of personalised stories. Kucirkova et al.'s (2013) study of how a mother created a story with her child based on their family holiday showed how easy it is to use these apps to make both reading and writing experiences responsive to 'in the moment' story sharing. The flexible incorporation of text, images and sounds into one storyboard, means that written, audio and visual alterations can occur instantly through sharing together. This digital story-making was also shown to enhance the embodied interaction between the child and the mother – their gestures, movements, touch and talk. The iPad device, and the multimodal communication it offered, e.g. picture, voice recordings and typed text, shaped and extended the literacy experience of mother and child together.

Interestingly, a study across seven European countries aimed at exploring young children and their families' experience with digital technology showed that digital technologies are an important, but not dominant, part of children's home life (Chaudron et al., 2015). Digital play appeared to be balanced with many other activities, including outdoor play and playing with non-digital toys. Young children used digital activities to extend their non-digital interests, showing the important inter-play that exists in children's digital and non-digital activities. An important finding was that children's reading and writing skills influenced the quality and levels of their digital interactions, demonstrating that access to digital technologies is predicated on traditional literacies and, therefore, inseparable from them.

Home for the majority of children is a rich site for technological experiences, but families also need support in how best to support these literacy encounters. Early years settings and schools have an active role to play in promoting creative and educational uses of digital technologies as well as addressing safety matters at home with parents and carers. It is recommended that information materials should be given to parents outlining the positive benefits of engagement with digital technology and supporting them in making decisions about the type of technology to use with their children (Chaudron et al., 2015).

Literacy play with touchscreens and apps

Various studies have shown how young children are able to bring their interactive skills and the digital knowledge gained from home into early years settings and classrooms. The widespread use of iPads and tablets means that toddlers and young children are familiar with touchscreens and apps as part of their everyday play with family members and friends. However, the value that these technologies have in helping children to develop other literacies, such as print-based literacy, is dependent on the type of app that children are using. For example, Neumann et al.'s (2017) study looking at the relationships between young children's home use of tablets and their growing literacy skills (print awareness, print knowledge, sound knowledge) discovered that children who used different writing and drawing apps more often at home had greater print awareness and letter and sound knowledge than children who used touchscreens less frequently for writing. They concluded that compared to gaming apps, literacy apps may possess certain features that engage children in typing and writing activities and, therefore, may be more useful for fostering emergent literacy.

Price et al. (2015) also looked at how very young children use iPad drawing apps by comparing children's digital mark-making to finger-painting activities using traditional materials. The iPads supported children's continuous touch-based interactions; children could make more marks and complete 'colouring in' finger-painting tasks quicker than using paint on paper as they didn't have to return to the paint palette to interrupt the 'flow'. More variation in touch movement was also observed as there was little resistance from the glass screen. Children were, therefore, able to increase speed and make quick back and forth, as well as circular movements with ease, and also vary the size of the marks being made. This smooth and continual finger movement provides a foundation for mark-making with other tools, such as pens or pencils and supports the forming of letter shapes. However, the material limitations of iPads were also noted, as the varied sensory experiences that children gained from playing with the physical paints was considerable. These are useful findings for educators to contemplate when they are selecting resources to support literacy. The materially affective relationship between the child and mark-making materials (both digital and non-digital) needs to be considered in order to support rich sensory as well as transformative intra-activity within writing play.

Extensive studies into the potential of iPads for classroom-based early literacy learning show that the portability and touch-responsive interface of iPads have the effect of stimulating children's concentration and engagement with early literacy learning when children use them both alone and in collaboration with others (Flewitt et al., 2015). However, the properties of the apps loaded onto iPads and the possibilities they offer children to be creative players has a salient effect on the quality of the literacy they experience. Open-content apps, for example storytelling and drawing, that require problem solving and creative contributions, engage children in deep levels of concentration and learning. Whereas apps with closed content, for example, alphabet games designed for children to repeatedly practise names and sounds, and procedural apps that do not encourage collaboration between players or ways to extend play through open-ended challenges, are less likely to be played with for very long (Flewitt et al., 2015; Marsh et al., 2015; Cowan, 2019). App design also needs scrutiny due to the lack of diversity and representation on offer for children. There is a call on app producers to consider not only cultural diversity, but other kinds of diversity too, to avoid limiting young children's engagement and imagination (Marsh et al., 2020). Designers should be consulting with young children as a way of understanding how their creativity can be cultivated; how they respond to characters and scenarios that both represent their lives and extend their experience of diverse worlds.

Digital stories and digital books

Reading for pleasure is essential and digital books can support the enjoyment and enthusiasm necessary to motivate young children to read. To support teachers and early years educators, Kucirkova et al. (2017) have created a tool to help select digital books to use with young children. When making choices they suggest that educators look for digital books that are age-appropriate, related to literacy (i.e. reading and writing rather than other activities), are simple, clear and intuitive to use. They have also developed an evaluative scale to assess the quality of engagement that occurs when children are using digital books. This scale focuses on children's affective engagement (their feelings and behaviour), shared engagement (collaboration and shared experience), sustained engagement (concentrated attention and focus) and creative engagement (levels of immersion in the book and possibility thinking).

As well as readers of digital books, young children can be creators of digital stories. This type of digital play provides young children with new and varied opportunities to make meaning, share ideas and create narratives together (Fleer, 2018b). For example, creating animated stories with children fosters creative multimodal storytelling. Importantly, for this type of digital play to be successful it needs scaffolding and instruction from teachers and educators, as well as a shared goal between all participants (both adult and children). For effective digital storytelling, adults should model how to use equipment and invite dialogue with children, both descriptive and predictive (Undheim and Jernes, 2020). Adult choices are also important in selecting the most effective materials needed to produce animated books, including physical materials such as clay, paint and paper and musical instruments, as well as the necessary digital tools, such as sound and video recording equipment. The case study below illustrates how Karim, an early years teacher, supports Alex to narrate and create his own personal story using an iPad app and an interactive whiteboard.

Case Study

Creating a Digital Text

Five-year-old Alex enjoys taking photos of his lively puppy using his father's phone. He shows his dad a succession of photos illustrating the puppy playing with a ball in a cardboard box. His parents add these to the digital learning journey that they share with his school to show his interest in photography.

At school the following week, his educator, Karim asks Alex if he would like to share his photos with the class. Alex enthusiastically talks about his dog as Karim displays the photos on the interactive whiteboard. The other children enjoy looking at the photos of Alex's dog playing in the box and this provokes other children to animatedly talk about their pets, showing great involvement and interest in this topic. Karim decides that it would be a great idea to capture this enthusiasm and later suggests to Alex that they could make a book using an iPad app.

The iPad app facilitates a discussion between Karim and Alex about which photos should be selected and which order they should appear in. This dialogue enables them to recount the story, enabling Karim to help Alex to sequence the course of events. The app facilitates interactivity, enabling them to change their choices and change the order with relative ease, facilitating further dialogue as choices are made. After the photos are selected, the app enables Alex to add his choice of audio. Alex decides to talk to some of the photos, adding dialogue to explain that his dog is trying to find his ball. For other photos, he chooses to add some music from the app menu. Karim encourages him to rehearse what he wants to say, before showing Alex how to record his voice. Karim is able to show Alex how to erase recordings that go 'wrong' and re-record these, illustrating the importance of rehearsal when creating new content.

At all times, Karim encourages Alex to make his own choices. He appreciates that this is Alex's story, and he can tell it as he wishes. He does not mind that the order is slightly out of sequence and the audio is not perfect. He understands that this is Alex's creation. When the story has been captured, he asks Alex if he wants to make a cover for the digital storyboard. Alex thinks that this is a great idea, suggesting that he draws a picture of his dog for the front cover. Karim suggests using a painting 'app' to do this, enabling Alex to trace his finger along the screen, selecting tools and colours to create his drawing. Finally, Karim suggests that they think of a title for the book. Alex keenly suggests the name of his dog 'Radar'. Karim suggests that they also need to include the name of the author on the front cover, provocatively asking who this might be. Alex smiles and says, 'me'.

Alex proudly reads his story to his friends at the end of the day, using the interactive whiteboard. This prompts the other children to ask whether they can make one tomorrow to which Alex responds that he can 'show them how to do it'.

Reflective questions

How does the app selected by Karim, support Alex to retell his story?

How does the technology facilitate Alex's storytelling in a way that is more challenging using pens and paper?

Hybrid literacy play and digital toys

One of the key elements of children's play in the digital age is that at home and in other learning spaces, it is impossible to separate traditional play from engagement with technologies (Edwards, 2018). The meaning making that children engage in when they play is dependent on the materials to hand (both digital and non-digital). Children blend their play, travelling between on and offline contexts, creating a hybridity between the two (Burnett et al., 2014). We have seen this in the mark-making and storytelling activities discussed above where there is a coming together of literacies within hybrid play spaces. This fluid movement across boundaries of space and time where children explore the properties of digital and non-digital things was not possible in the pre-digital era (Marsh, 2018). The rise of digital and robot toys, specifically designed so that they function by being connected to the internet, is an example of how this hybrid play connects the non-digital and the digital.

As an example of this, Marsh (2017) demonstrates the synergies that exist between young children's online and offline play in her study of one three-year-old girl, Amy, and her play with a toy Furby that was controlled by an app on a tablet. Both the tablet and Furby are moved around in Amy's play, adjusted and controlled as she moves back and forth between each. She is observed moving her fingers from screen to toy, pressing buttons, waving and talking both to the screen and the Furby. Amy also introduces other toys, demonstrating the flow of connections that exist between the physical object (here, the Furby) and its online domain (the app). These connections are creatively fostered by Amy as she infolds this technology into her play in flexible ways.

Kewalramani et al.'s (2020) research also explored this blurring of digital and non-digital environments by studying how children across four countries interacted with IoToys (physical toys that link to the internet) in early years settings. They found that these toys offered play that was multidirectional and multimodal. The toys gave children messages of praise and encouragement and stimulated collaboration and interactivity between children as they problem solved and learnt skills from each other. The children were able to personalise their interactions, giving them a sense of autonomy and increasing creative play. Like the storytelling apps discussed in the case study above, it was shown that guidance and support by the early years teacher through questioning and building children's confidence was significant in the communicative gains that children could achieve.

Other IoToys, uniquely robot toys, have particular interactive potential due to their physical make-up – their material form. The key feature of many of these robot toys is their human or animal-like shape and the multimodal communication behaviour they exhibit: 'shared gaze', responsive gestures and interactive movements. Vulchanova et al. (2017) after reviewing current research into robot technologies concluded that, to support children's language and literacy, any future developments of robot aids need to exploit the benefits that come from these anthropomorphic features (the human characteristics of communication). We are not recommending the replacement of human interaction with robots here! But children playing with these toys are able to take control and lead interactions, and in the same way that children can explore communication with others in small world and role play, robot toys provide imaginative scenarios from which to practise and develop their multimodal communication with 'another'.

Pedagogical foundations and digital literacies

The focus of this chapter has been on how digital and non-digital materials can come together as part of a successful pedagogy of meaning making. This means that educators need to hold onto the features of play that have developed from its philosophical foundations and understand how digital materials can extend and enhance these features. Cowan's (2019) research into digital practices in Swedish preschools inspired by Reggio Emilia approaches, demonstrates that a strong pedagogical foundation can lead educators' digital choices in meaningful ways. The educators in Cowan's study viewed digital communication as another language within the 'hundred languages' philosophy (see Chapter 1). Training spaces for these educators included both digital and 'traditional' tools in order to demonstrate how to generate communicative encounters with children. Malleable materials and musical instruments were located near an iPad with motion-capture software, and a screen was projected on walls to encourage explorations of sound, vision and narrative. These practices demonstrated the communicative and multimodal potential these educators felt digital technologies offered young children.

In developing digital literacies with young children, adult choices matter – these choices should be based on secure and well-articulated knowledge of play pedagogy. Close observation of how young children engage with digital technologies as they play demonstrates that children move fluidly between different devices and materials, travelling from the non-digital to the digital world and back again. This creates multiple literacy possibilities. Educators have an essential role in introducing young children to digital technologies alongside other materials to extend literacies; this is imperative for countering disadvantage created as a result of limited access to good quality digital tools.

Practice ideas

Here are some ideas that you may find useful in creating digital literacy opportunities for young children:

- GoPros. Children can wear GoPros to capture their experiences while building outdoors using found objects; this could then be turned into a documentary to share with parents and carers.
- iPads. Children can film their small world play, and transfer these into storytelling apps to share with friends.
- Audio books. Very young children can mime the actions of songs and story book characters as they listen to audio recorded stories.
- Digital microscopes. These can be used to capture close up images of the natural world. Children can then draw these images and publish these as a digital book.
- QR codes. Children can go on a treasure hunt by scanning the QR codes for clues helping them to find out where to go next to find the hidden treasure. These clues could relate to letter sounds, topics or themes that are being explored.

In Summary

- Digital technology supports young children's literacy knowledge and skills by extending their interactive communication, creative storytelling, mark-making and engagement with reading.
- Children play with digital technologies in a fluid way: they bring together digital and non-digital materials and move between on and offline spaces.
- To enhance digital literacy opportunities, educators should model and scaffold digital literacy learning and select quality digital resources to be used alongside traditional materials.

Having reflected on the content of the chapter, here are some **discussion questions** to share with colleagues.

1. Have you observed children interacting/intra-acting with iPad apps/digital technologies? What are their favourites? How are you able to use their enthusiasm and interests to connect digital play with other types of traditional play?
2. How do digital technologies affect the way that you interact with children? Do they decrease or increase the tendency for interactions with peers and adults?

3. How could you use digital tools to enhance young children's hybrid play (where they bring digital and non-digital toys/materials together)? What could you do to develop children's communication and movement when using digital tools both inside and outside?

Further recommended reading

DigiLitEY (2020) http://digilitey.eu/

This website represents the work of an EU-funded initiative to create an interdisciplinary network to advance understandings of young children's digital literacy and multimodal practices in the new media age. There is a large quantity of resources and reports with guidance for educators created by the various working groups to support the best digital practices with young children.

Marsh, S. (2018) Childhood in the digital age. In S. Powell and K. Smith (Eds.), An Introduction to Early Childhood Studies, pp. 53–63. London: Sage.

In this chapter, Jackie Marsh introduces us to the influences that affect childhood in the digital age and argues that young children's digital play can promote creativity and communication with friends, families and communities. Marsh takes a measured approach in her discussion, recognising the limitations and risks of digital technology as well as its potentialities.

7

'WE'RE GOING ON A BEAR HUNT': LANGUAGE AND LITERACIES IN OUTDOOR PLAY

This chapter will

- explore the significance of outdoor play in developing children's literacies;
- highlight potential outdoor learning opportunities;
- consider some of the barriers to outdoor play and learning and how to overcome them;
- enable you to evaluate the role that adults have in promoting outdoor learning opportunities for children's literacy play.

Outdoor learning has long been a tradition in early childhood education because of the wide-ranging benefits that it has in supporting children's learning and development. In Chapter 1, we considered how Froebel's work emphasises the importance of the children's garden or 'kindergarten' in helping to 'cultivate' engaged learners (Tovey, 2017). Working with young children in the early twentieth century and inspired by Froebel's ideas, Margaret and Rachel Macmillan were also influential in promoting the importance of fresh air and exercise when seeking to meet children's physical needs (Jarvis, 2013). The outdoors offers an ever-changing sensory environment with space and freedom that affords children opportunities to develop literacies that are hard to recreate indoors. Many of the benefits of learning outdoors focus on young children's holistic development – the combination of sensory, physical, social and emotional learning experience. These elements are important for all aspects of children's learning; however, this chapter will specifically explore the uniqueness and potential of outdoor play in supporting early literacies.

'Outdoors' is a term used to describe the physical environment for learning; however, there are a range of ways in which educators perceive this term.

Differences in interpreting the value of the outdoors arise because of underlying values and principles that are associated with each setting and these have the potential to influence the ways that educators approach their work (Waite, 2020). The impact of these values and principles mean that provision varies. In some cases, outdoor classrooms replicate indoor provision, whilst in others, the outdoors is used as a space for more dynamic physical activity where children can expend their energy. Some settings have access to more natural and 'wild' areas of space and can afford children free-flow or timetabled sessions within this natural environment, such as forest school sessions. Other settings have limited access to nature. Whatever the environment, approaches to learning in the outdoors are all influenced by the degree to which independence for children is fostered by educators in settings. Enabling children to move through different spaces that afford different potentialities in play and literacy help them to make choices. Having 'agency' and choice about where to take their learning is key, so free-flow access within different environments, including the outdoors, is crucial in supporting motivation and focus as children enact literacy through their play.

Reflection

What have you experienced in terms of the values and attitudes towards learning in the outdoors? Have you observed any restrictions or limits placed on outdoor spaces? Is there potential to open these up to enable greater access to more natural environments?

Communicative interactions outdoors

Fostering agency for children when they are outdoors, supports children's literacy learning because learning to use language is influenced by children's interactions with their environments. As explored in Chapter 3, when children play, their play is 'story-like' as they make decisions about characters, plots and settings (Streelansky, 2019). Children who can interact with others and with materials within natural environments, are able to become more involved in open-ended play for longer periods (Richardson and Murray, 2017). These experiences enable children to express themselves, vocalise and project their voices as they build their confidence over time.

Trialling different pitches and sounds within particular soundscapes and outside spaces enables children to communicate and create their own 'stories' which help them to make sense of their worlds and connect with those of others. Some of these story ideas are derived from media (Wohlwend, 2017) as well as other cultural experiences within their individual worlds such as routines, food, celebrations, etc. In outdoor environments, children create and recreate stories based on these cultural experiences, incorporating the different properties of natural objects such as sticks, stones, mud, grass, ditches and trees. The natural landscape offers scope to transform or influence children's play and assists them in utilising natural resources as symbols. Children are adept at using resources at their disposal to 'be' something else. They use these as toys or replacement objects, which they can use to communicate with, as well as to imagine new possibilities and directions for their play. For example, a stick has huge potential as a light sabre, a wand or even as a doorway, while a stone might be money, food or even a fairy. Playing with these natural objects offers a way for children to develop their play themes and has a central role within a freeing, natural outdoor environment that is rich with potential. As outlined in previous chapters, for young children one object can stand in as a replacement for another – a process of representative thinking that importantly underpins reading and writing. The symbolic potential of materials in the outside environment is infinite, providing children with multiple ways to experience these aspects of literacy.

Research by Harwood and Collier (2017) emphasises how sticks and other objects become highly significant for children as they engage in literacy play. Children actively 'think with sticks' as they create stories and texts that incorporate the stick as a friend, or as a force for change (p. 337). Environments that have natural objects available are significant in fostering imaginative play and literacy. Play is, of itself, a form of literacy that facilitates an existence that goes 'beyond print' as children become one with their environments (Harwood and Collier, 2017, p. 339). While natural objects can also be mark-making materials, being at one with the environment, creating stories and being in the moment, sensing, feeling, touching and smelling the natural world is a fundamental literacy experience. Valuing the novelty, surprise and wonder of the outdoors is important in enabling children to create stories and texts incidentally. The following vignette highlights how incidental experiences in the outdoors offer rich potential for children's play and literacy learning:

━Vignette━

Literacy opportunities in the natural environment

A group of five-year-old children are playing in some woodland adjacent to their school playground on the edge of a larger piece of scrubland. They are looking at an owl pellet they have just found with their teaching Assistant, Sam. Sam is encouraging them to think about what it might be, and the children eagerly offer their responses ranging from a rabbit dropping to a piece of stick. Sam gently encourages them further, by asking them to explain why they think what they do. She encourages them to use different vocabulary to explain the reasons for their ideas. The children listen carefully to each other, eager to find out what the strange looking thing is. Sam explains that this owl pellet has been produced by an owl after they have finished eating their food. She explains that owls aren't able to digest all of the bones, hair or fur of the animals they eat. She introduces the children to specialist scientific language such as 'pellet', 'digestion', 'regurgitated' and 'dissection'.

Next, Sam suggests that they go on an owl hunt to find tracks, a possible nest and evidence of the food that the owl was eating. This requires the children to use instructions with each other and also to communicate at a distance. Sam encourages them to find their own unique way to communicate through the trees and bushes; a distinctive call so that they can keep communicating. The children discover that they also manage to make their own marks in the mud to indicate where they have been. This leads to a game where they follow each other to a hiding place.

The significance of outdoor literacies

The literacy in this vignette was 'liberated' due to the outdoor space but was also inspired by the natural environment. The outdoors is shown here to be a place where children can initiate and lead their own learning rather than being led by adults; however, the educator has a vital role in introducing new vocabulary and modelling ways of speaking and listening. Of course, these spaces and places need to be inspected for safety, but opportunities within outdoor environments have the potential to increase the quality of children's language (Richardson and Murray, 2017).

Children's interactions within a natural environment appear to have significant benefits for the quality of their expressive language, increasing the usage of verbs, adjectives and exclamations (Richardson and Murray, 2017). As children immerse themselves within their own worlds, making choices and decisions about who to be, how to act or what to say, they naturally try out new words or make up words. They use the language of those around them, which appears to have an expansive effect on the amount of 'doing' and 'naming' words. As children become more involved and excited in their play, this appears to heighten their vocalisations which impacts on the pitch and tone of their expressions (Richardson and Murray, 2017). Trying out and developing the use of voice is experienced through these vocalisations and this excitement acts to further fuel engagement and drives children to continue developing their play themes.

Reflection

What are the considerations that you would need to make if you were to support children learning in the outdoors? What are the benefits and what risks might you face? How would you overcome these?

As children expand their vocabulary, use their voice and vocalise through interacting with their play companions, as well as move through different outdoor environments they are able to explore new narratives and ideas. This allows them to express their experiences, emotions, fears, fantasies and ideas as they negotiate rules, turns and roles. As these expressions are enacted as stories, they become 'action texts' (Wohlwend, 2017). These action texts or stories have no need for paper or mark-making materials. They are alive as embodiments of children's thoughts. Jarvis' (2007) research examining the narratives of four- to six-year-old children playing football outdoors found that these action texts were infused with both social and symbolic significance. Young children were learning to work together with peers to understand and interpret the actions of others within the game. Listening, predicting, responding appropriately and expressing responses that are congruent with the subject matter are all vital components of learning to be literate.

Playing in natural outdoor environments such as woodland, forests, heaths, grasslands and fields hold great potential for children to transform their thoughts into 'modes of representation' (Streelansky, 2019, p. 95). Sometimes this means observing as a story unfolds and is altered or developed as children engage in 'storying rather than storytelling' (Wohlwend, 2017, p. 66). They work together to make decisions about where the story is taking place, what is going to happen in the story and who is going to be what character in the story. Sometimes these decisions are responsive 'in the moment' decisions, other times, they arise from other influences such as media, experiences or ideas from previous play episodes.

Children need their educators to notice how they are responding within these environments and educators need to be open to possible ways to support, enhance or develop the play. This means carefully observing how children are responding. Educators need to be alert in different outdoor environments to how children are playing to sensitively know when to interact with them and when not to as this won't necessarily enhance the quality of children's outdoor play (Fisher, 2016). As playing outside is itself a form of communication involving different modes or acts of expression, it requires educators to sensitively intervene in response to the affordances the environment offers for children's play.

Children often think aloud as they play. The play decisions that children make outside are assisted by using the language available to them to express their thoughts. They talk themselves through their thinking and as their peers and educators respond to these vocalisations, they are able to learn the impact that they have on the world. This further encourages children to use language to respond and it also develops their ability to socially and emotionally adapt their responses. These experiences help them to develop their relationships with others; their emotional literacy.

The rich literacies that are associated with play outlined above suggest that educators need to find ways to enable children to have lots of opportunities to involve themselves in play within natural settings. Children should also be able to move into and around a variety of outdoor spaces, including being able to flow freely between indoor and outside environments. In the case study that follows, you can read how Ben is able to find creative ways of supporting children's learning outside in an environment that has limited access to outside spaces (Natural England, 2016).

Case Study

Supporting Children Learning Literacies within a Restricted Outdoor Environment

Ben is a preschool educator. He has observed that the three- and four-year-old children in his setting particularly enjoy the story, *We're Going on a Bear Hunt* by Michael Rosen. This book is about a family that go in search of a bear and encounter several different environmental conditions such as long grass, thick mud, swirling snow and a dark forest. Ben wants to find a way to enable the children to experience this story as a way to support their developing language and literacy. He sees that there is an opportunity to develop their sense of rhyme and rhythm, to experiment with wonderful adjectives, to use the pitch and tone of their voices in different ways, to recite the story together and to act out and experience the different materials and conditions within the story. He believes that these are all really important in enabling the children to love stories and reading. However, Ben is challenged by the environment that he works in. His preschool has limited outdoor space, hardly any is natural, and he doesn't have any access to any woodland as it is located within a built-up urban area.

Ben decides to use some old trays that are in the cupboard to create a series of different conditions and to take the trays outside. He explains to the children that he wants to find things to put in the trays so that they can act out the story together. The children eagerly make suggestions such as 'digging up mud from my garden', 'ice from the freezer for snow', 'making Lego trees' and they even suggest that they use the toy bear from the home corner to be the bear character and make a cave for him out of a blanket and a chair. Despite the rain, they put on the 'all-in-ones' and wellington boots and eagerly rope off a corner of the car park in the outdoor area to keep them safe. They set up the trays on the tarmac. Ben lays down some old blankets and rugs in between the trays to protect the children's feet and they eagerly kick off their boots and socks before touching and stepping into the different conditions. Ben stands back and observes them delightfully exploring before entering into the play himself. He leads a retelling of the story and the children eagerly join in with him, chanting the words and giggling as they invent new obstacles for the bear.

Barriers to literacy learning in outdoor spaces

Educators need to find ways to overcome barriers to outdoor literacy learning for young children, as Ben did in the case study above. Children who have lots of outdoor experiences are far more likely to spend time out of doors connecting with and having more positive attitudes towards the environment when they become adults (Broom, 2017). However, children are spending less time outdoors than ever before (Bilton, 2010), with one government report suggesting that there are social inequalities regarding children's access to the outdoors (Natural England, 2016). The attitudes of parents towards risk impact on their children is a significant consideration for educators. Some children don't have the desire to play out of doors as a result of our modern lifestyles and anxieties about the dangers (Bilton, 2010). Some of these anxieties arise as a result of fear held by the adults who care for young children, rather than the children themselves. They emerge from worries about traffic, strangers, bullying or other forms of harm. Concerns about the weather or health and safety can, therefore, hamper children's learning (Bilton, 2020). There is a correlation between the perceived risks that parents associate with the outdoor play scenarios presented to them, and the increased level of risk aversion shown by their children (Murray and Williams, 2020). However, if we wrap children in 'cotton wool', they never learn to manage their own risks. Stoking this 'culture of fear' means that children's freedom is being curbed (Furedi, 2008), so educators have a responsibility in supporting children to experience being in the outdoors while in their care. If children have limited access to the outdoors, particularly access to nature and natural environments, they may experience what Louv (2005) has termed, 'nature deficit disorder'. He claims that denying children access to nature may contribute to conditions such as obesity, attention-deficit disorder, isolation and depression. The implication of Louv's work is that educators need to work hard with children and families to support them in understanding the benefits of playing in the outdoors.

In the case study above, Ben experienced several barriers to fostering play in the outdoors. The children had limited access to outdoor space, and this lacked natural features such as mud, grass, sticks and stones. This meant that he had to bring these materials to the children. He also had to consider health and safety of the children in accessing a part of land not often used by the children by roping this off for their use. He had to consider the weather, but this did not deter him as the setting had 'all-in-one' rainproof overalls. However, despite these challenges, Ben believed that these experiences are important. Having this space for his children to be out of doors, experiencing storytelling in this way, was an engaging and motivating way for them to be learning. They were able to engage more actively in the outdoors than they would have been able to indoors and there were significant benefits for their ability to use language, express themselves, connect words and experiences in order to build meaning and to participate in the enjoyment of shared storytelling in a meaningful way. Involving the children in the decision making fostered their motivation to be involved in the experience. Ben was not concerned about the weather; he had the right clothing available. He was also conscious of hazards in roping off a safe area for the children to be in while enabling them the freedom to explore the different trays in a sensory way and to take risks to try something new. Children had the choice about whether to be involved or not. Children need to experience opportunities such as this to learn how to manage their own risks. This is not to expose them to hazardous, dangerous risks, but instead, to risks that enable them to make decisions and choices about where and how they play. Tovey (2007, p. 101) argues that there is a 'danger' in creating 'risk-free environments' because they lead to children becoming risk averse and uninspired. Instead, we should offer safe environments in which children can explore and take measured risks. Children need to be able to experiment with different modes and communicative practices (Streelansky, 2019).

Communicating in different ways, therefore, needs to be encouraged by educators, which may require an element of risk taking on the part of children and their educators. All exploratory play requires some risk and without it, children may miss opportunties to develop literacies both inside and out. Children need opportunities to be able to seek thrills, experience joy and fear and learn what it feels like to be in and out of control (Tovey, 2007; Sandseter, 2009). They need to find the language to describe these feelings and emotions and to have opportunities to talk about these.

Reflective questions

What risks were the children taking in the bear hunt case study?

What are the benefits for the children in the scenario?

How did this play benefit the children's imagination, language use and their understanding of storytelling?

Loose parts

Outdoor environments offer unique access to all sorts of differently textured natural objects and loose parts (Nicholson, 1971). Loose parts are open-ended materials that foster imaginative and creative forms of play and outdoor environments offer a diverse range of loose parts for children to play with. As well as being wonderful inspiration for children's imaginative role play, storying, experiences and ideas, loose parts also offer enormous potential to capture narratives through mark-making and writing. Sticks, twigs, pebbles, grass, leaves and stones can be used not only to make marks in sand, mud, dust and water but also can be placed in various configurations to represent letters or signs. The following case study shows how Yuan's attachment to his magic stick inspired Jeannie to reconsider her provision in her nursery setting:

┌─ Case Study ─┐

Supporting play with 'Loose Parts

On his walk one day to his nursery setting, Yuan discovers a stick that has landed on the path after a particularly windy night. He runs towards it and picks it up exclaiming that it is a powerful wand. He waves it in the air, pointing it towards the oncoming cars and shouting loudly, 'disappearo!'. In his mind, the stick has magical powers that act on the world. Once he arrives at his destination, he carries his wand into the nursery where he safely places it in one of his wellington boots and runs off to meet his friends. A short while later, his nursery educator Jeannie picks up the stick and places it onto a high shelf for safekeeping.

Later that morning, the children play outdoors for a short while and Yuan asks for his wand. He wants to include it in his imaginative play, but he is told that 'sticks aren't allowed in the outdoor play area'. Yuan is sad but soon gets distracted by his friends; however, Jeannie notices Yuan's disappointed response and later that day shares her thoughts with the lead educator. She explains that she thinks it would be a good idea to have an area of the outdoors for children to access more 'loose parts' play to foster their imaginative learning. The lead educator is concerned about safety, stating that 'sticks are dangerous so we can't have them in the setting'. In response, Jeannie asks for permission to develop a small uncultivated area of land on the edge of the hardstanding into a natural play area and assures the lead educator that the area will be supervised at all times. Permission is granted and some months later, Jeannie is proud that this area is one of the most popular areas in the setting. She has worked hard to help the other educators in the setting to understand the importance of 'loose parts play' through sharing articles and holding discussions about the value of it.

Several months on, children now have access to large and small sticks, pebbles, stones, grass, trees and mud. They use them as objects within their play. They construct with the stones, balance on the logs, arrange the pebbles and dig in the mud. All of the educators have attended professional learning opportunities led by Jeannie on the value of natural resources. Jeannie has noticed that the children ask to play in this area in all weathers and that through the months, they have engaged in all sorts of different types of imaginative play, fostering storytelling and role taking. Their educators no longer prevent children from playing with sticks because the children have been part of the discussions to ensure that no one gets hurt and they understand that there are rules to keep everyone safe. The sticks are now a welcome sight, used to build, construct, mark make and imagine with.

In the case study above, Jeannie noticed that the children in her care were enthused by incorporating natural objects into their play and actively sought to create an environment that would enable them to have access to these resources, despite the barriers that she faced. Carefully assessing risks and weighing these up against the potential benefits for children's literacy learning enabled the educators in this setting to appreciate the importance of enabling children to access materials and objects that foster engagement in playful literacies.

Reflective questions

How did Jeannie's careful observations of Yuan lead to a change of provision for the children in this setting?

What benefits are there in using found and natural materials to support early literacies?

Role of adults in promoting literacies in the outdoors

The focus of this chapter has been to look at how outdoor natural environments support children's literacy learning. It has examined how play within the outdoors supports children in using and interpreting language as a way to foster meaning-making with both peers and adults. It has also considered the importance of the natural world in fostering children's play and imaginative thinking in order to create literary texts as well as to offer potential opportunities to make marks and engage in creating texts. The implications are that educators need to be able to understand and advocate for the provision of outdoor literacy learning opportunities. They have a role in supporting others to appreciate the importance of play in children's literacy learning.

Educators need to look for opportunities to facilitate children's exploratory language, to enable and encourage them to play with their voices and to feel safe to try out different ways of talking and expressing themselves. Finding resources to support this exploration is key. There are many inexpensive amplifiers and communication devices that can be easily used to enable children to explore in the outdoors. For example, a hand or a piece of cardboard can easily form a trumpet to help project their voices. Drainpipes or tubing also offer scope for children to be able to hide and to still communicate by talking through the tube. This activity could even be extended to morse code-type communication with taps and bangs to communicate certain actions or commands. Mobile digital tools such as cameras and GoPros can be moved into different environments by children in their play with the potential to record outdoor learning events and then be shown and shared with others, encouraging explanation and reiteration.

Adults have an important role as modellers of communication and playing with children (when invited) is a way to truly appreciate the rules of outdoor engagement. Being part of the action enables you to know when to support and 'scaffold' (Vygotsky, 1978) children's language and literacies. Understanding when children might need some encouragement or help to manage something new and to take managed risks can be empowering and lead to rich learning potential. Sometimes, this may mean that adults need to be prepared to follow the children's lead.

Practice ideas

Here are some ideas that you may find useful in developing children's access to the outdoors to develop their language and literacy learning within your setting:

- Seek support from leaders and managers for regular access to natural areas for children to play in to foster the quality of their expressive language. This may require some persuasion and negotiation! Use these areas to sing songs, perform action songs, dance.
- Find ways to enable children to have free-flow access to outdoor spaces in your setting as much as possible for extended periods of time.
- Ensure that your setting has clothing that protects children from the elements so that they can play out of doors in all weathers and experience the changing environments.
- Create different 'mini environments' in your outdoor space that introduces children to natural and human-made materials, textures and objects, inspiring them to explore, create and imagine new possibilities for literacy play, including mark-making.
- Consider ways of re-enacting stories in the outdoors and involve the children in making decisions about props and costumes. Think about what they could use to project their voices (microphones, paper cones, megaphones).
- Have a variety of sound-making equipment available for using outdoors. Long cardboard or plastic tubes offer great potential for children to communicate with each other in different ways.
- Use digital tools to record sounds outside and listen back together noticing the sound scape made by both humans and animals.
- Try setting out a tray of water and some brushes and brooms for children to make different marks on a dry area of tarmac or spread out some damp sand for them to create marks or different landscapes. Mud would also work.

In summary

- Playing outdoors encourages children to communicate and use language in diverse ways, and practise literacy skills. Educators need to be aware of the barriers to this and to find ways to alleviate the concerns of adults as well as to encourage children to be outdoors.
- Educators should encourage young children to engage in loose parts play. Having a range of natural materials and resources available will help to extend children's imagination and symbolic play.

- Children need opportunities in outside spaces to vocalise, shout, perform and create action texts that help them to story, imagine, predict and represent their inner imaginative worlds.

Having reflected on the content of the chapter, here are some **discussion questions** to help you in planning for young children's literacies in outside environments:

1. Consider how children can have free-flow access to natural environments and loose parts within the outdoors. What risk assessments might you have to do before they are able to access the outdoors and how will you support them to take healthy risks that support their learning?
2. Have a shared conversation about sticks and den building. What materials could you source to enable children to make large constructions from natural materials?
3. How do you help children to learn new vocabulary to describe their experiences in the outdoors?

Further recommended reading

Nicholson, S. (1971) *Theory of Loose Parts: How Not to Cheat Children.* Available online: https://media.kaboom.org/docs/documents/pdf/ip/Imagination-Playground-Theory-of-Loose-Parts-Simon-Nicholson.pdf (Accessed 29.03.21).

Tovey, H. (2017) *Outdoor Play and Exploration.* Available online: www.froebel.org.uk/training-and-resources/pamphlets (Accessed 20.03.21). The Froebel Trust has a great selection of free pamphlets available and this one by Helen Tovey shows how Froebel's vision is still highly relevant for us today. There are some wonderful images and ideas to support you in planning for children's literacy in the outdoors.

This seminal paper explains why loose parts are so important in supporting children to explore the world and be creative as future environmental citizens.

8

CURRICULUM CONVERSATIONS: HOW THE CURRICULUM CAN SUPPORT LITERACIES AND PLAY

This chapter will

- introduce you to early childhood curriculum debates around literacy and play;
- consider how literacies and play are framed within the Early Years Foundation Stage;
- familiarise you with international curricula approaches and the opportunities they offer for participatory play and literacy;
- help you to understand terms such as 'child-initiated' and 'adult led' in planning literacy activity with children;
- support you in reclaiming the playful adult role in early years classrooms and settings.

Early childhood is highly politicised and curriculum debates are framed by societal values and government ideologies. Political ideologies make their presence felt through the policies and curricular frameworks that are created in the form of statutory and non-statutory documentation that guide professionals with a responsibility to educate young children. In England and many other countries in the affluent northern hemisphere these documents aim to ensure that the stock of human capital (Wells, 2009) meets the needs of future global competition; in this way, the economy frames a future-orientated approach to early childhood language and literacy practices. These neoliberal views contrast with early childhood's long legacy of practice centred on the importance of enabling children to 'be' rather than 'become', which sees children as human beings rather than human 'becomings' (Qvortrup, 2009). Managing these conflicting values and ideologies causes tensions in early years educators' day-to-day decision making about how best to support young children in their care.

However, within all curricular frameworks and guidance, there is usually potential for influence and interpretation by educators that will affect the experiences that young children have. Young (2014) suggests that if we acknowledge the curriculum 'as a "structure" offering constraints and possibilities' (p. 8) we might be able to adapt this structure so that what we value as important knowledge for young children, and how we would like them to gain this knowledge, can be recognised and acted upon. The implication of Young's argument is that as educators of young children, there are choices that can be made whatever curriculum (as guidance) is on offer. As a starting point, educators need to examine the framework that they are 'given', and their own assumptions of what provision should look like that stems from this framework. This chapter will help you to critically engage in the curriculum debates by comparing three very different curricular approaches, supporting your understanding of how literacies and play are brought together in alternative ways, each one led by different ideologies and values.

To begin this critical engagement, consider this vignette of a young child playing with water. What 'literacies' do you see?

─Vignette─

Exploratory water play and emerging literacies

Samuel is 4 years old and is in the reception year (the first year of school in England). He is sitting next to a water tray that is placed on the ground with a small puddle of water in the bottom of the tray. Around the edge, the water has evaporated leaving the blue plastic to dry in the warm sunshine. There are objects in the water that is left, such as spades, paintbrushes, cups and sieves. Samuel dips his hand into the water and with a sweeping motion, scoops up the water. It runs straight through his fingers, splashing the outside of the tray. He watches the water 'disappear' as it flows back into the puddle at the bottom of the tray and the warmth of the sunshine evaporates any trace. After a while, Samuel uses his wet fingers to trace what seems to be a letter shape on the warm blue plastic tray. After a few seconds, it disappears. He tries different marks before taking off his socks and shoes and stands in the water tray. He gets into the water and surprised by the cold, he steps back out onto the paving stones. He notices the footprints left by his wet feet and fishes out a truck from the water tray. He uses this to make more marks on the paving stones, delighting as they evaporate and disappear from view.

┤ Reflective questions ├

Can you identify the literacies that Samuel is exploring through his water play?

What are your thoughts about the provision?

Why has the educator offered this experience for Samuel? What literacies appear to be valued in this setting?

In the vignette, you may have considered the importance for Samuel to engage in his own decision making, have opportunities to make marks, to tell stories, to create scenarios that recreate or play out different experiences or ideas, real or imagined. Your thoughts about this will be shaped by your beliefs and values about the role of the educator. This will most likely have been shaped by the policies and curriculum frameworks that you have experienced.

Do you view Samuel in this vignette as preparing to be a future literate citizen or already someone who has knowledge of different literacies? Perhaps your focus is on the knowledge that Samuel hasn't yet acquired to be able to be a literate person, or are you more aware of how you could affirm the literacies he is playing with now? Whatever your thoughts, Samuel was experiencing a play encounter that enabled him to initiate his own learning, make decisions about what he wanted to do next, and foster his own motivation and engagement – all significant in being and becoming with literacies. He was exploring what the water can do to support his developing understanding of the world around him. There was a whole world of imaginative possibilities developing in his head. As we have pointed out throughout this book, the possibilities of play in supporting children's literacies are endless. Our role as adults are crucial in fostering playful environments and the opportunities in which literacies can flourish. In the next section, we will first consider how the EYFS (DfE, 2021) shapes our values and principles as early years educators before moving on to consider two other alternative curricular frameworks: Te Whāriki and Reggio Emilia. We will then reconsider Samuel's water play again.

Literacies and play in the Early Years Foundation Stage

In the Early Years Foundation Stage (EYFS) (DfE, 2021), guiding principles determine the practice of all early years educators working in Ofsted registered settings in England. These guiding principles are:

- every child is a *unique child*, who is constantly learning and can be resilient, capable, confident and self-assured;
- children learn to be strong and independent through *positive relationships*;
- children learn and develop well in *enabling environments with teaching and support from adults*, who respond to their individual interests and needs and help them to build their learning over time. Children benefit from a strong partnership between practitioners and parents and/or carers;
- importance of *learning and development*. Children develop and learn at different rates ... The framework covers the education and care of all children in early years provision, including children with special educational needs and disabilities (SEND) (EYFS, 2021, p. 6).

These guiding principles emphasise that children's educational experiences between the ages of birth and five, need to be based on meeting their developmental learning needs through an approach that appreciates that care is as much a consideration as education, so that literacy learning can flourish. The importance of play in meeting these needs cannot be overstated and is explicitly acknowledged in the framework as 'essential for children's development' (EYFS, 2021, p. 16). Fostering close relationships with families and caregivers enable settings to closely meet children's communication, language and literacy needs throughout the EYFS.

The framework offers structured guidance that emphasises the ways in which adults might consider their provision. There is a focus on nurturing early learning dispositions, labelled 'characteristics of effective learning'. Educators are encouraged to consider how the children in their care are investigating and experiencing their environments and trying out new things (playing and exploring). They are encouraged to observe how children focus and keep trying and persisting with challenges as well as acknowledge their achievements (active learning) and whether they are able to express ideas, make links between them and solve problems to overcome adversity (creating and thinking critically) (EYFS, 2021, p. 16). Paying attention to the ways in which children are engaging in using communication and language supports each of the seven areas of learning.

The curricular expectations for early years education between birth and five are set out in the Early Years Foundation Stage Framework areas of learning (DfE, 2021). While 'it is up to providers to decide how they approach the curriculum' (DfE, 2021, p. 7), educators need to consider their provision across seven areas of learning that are termed either 'prime' or 'specific' areas of learning. The prime areas are considered to be a foundation for the more specific areas of learning which reinforce each of the prime areas. These areas are interrelated and so while the focus of this chapter is on literacy, we must not forget that children will be experiencing literacies within all of the areas of development.

The three prime areas of development are:

- communication and language,
- physical development, and
- personal, social and emotional development.

The four specific areas of learning are:

- literacy,
- mathematics,
- understanding the world, and
- expressive arts and design.

Communication and language as a prime area of learning and development underpins *all* of the areas of learning and development. As children interact and socialise with others, they are enabled to make meaning from these experiences and to build the very foundations of thinking. Adults have an important role in supporting these early interactions **as articulated in bold** in the following excerpt taken from the EYFS (DfE, 2021, p. 8).

The development of children's spoken language underpins all seven areas of learning and development. Children's back-and-forth interactions from an early age form the foundations for language and cognitive development. The number and quality of the conversations they have with adults and peers throughout the day in a **language-rich environment** is crucial. By **commenting on what children** are interested in or doing and echoing back what they say with new vocabulary added, practitioners will build children's language effectively. Reading frequently to children, and engaging them actively in stories, non-fiction, rhymes and poems, and then providing them with extensive opportunities to use and embed new words in a range of contexts, will give children the opportunity to thrive. Through conversation, storytelling and role play, where children share their ideas with support and modelling from their teacher, and sensitive questioning that invites them to elaborate, children become comfortable using a rich range of vocabulary and language structures.

The emphasis on listening, understanding and attention through the provision of a wide range of different experiences, opportunities and interactions that foster communication and language are assessed at the end of the EYFS in the reception year (DfE, 2021) where each child's expected level of development is assessed against two early learning goals for communication and language. Children are encouraged towards:

Listening, attention and understanding

- Listen attentively and respond to what they hear with relevant questions, comments and actions when being read to and during whole class discussions and small group interactions.
- Make comments about what they have heard and ask questions to clarify their understanding.
- Hold conversations when engaged in back-and-forth exchanges with their teacher and peers.

Speaking

- Participate in small group, class and one-to-one discussions, offering their own ideas, using recently introduced vocabulary.
- Offer explanations for why things might happen, making use of recently introduced vocabulary from stories, non-fiction, rhymes and poems when appropriate.
- Express their ideas and feelings about their experiences using full sentences, including use of past, present and future tenses and making use of conjunctions, with modelling and support from their teacher.

Early Learning Goals (DfE, 2021)

These 'early learning goals' are the benchmark against which each child's level of development is assessed. Their purpose is for teachers to 'make a judgement about whether an individual child is at the expected level of development' so that they can 'make a holistic best-fit judgement about a child's development and their readiness for year 1' (DfE, 2021, p. 11). While the DfE (2021) explicitly states that 'the ELGs should not be used as a curriculum' (p. 11), this statement indicates that the core purpose of the EYFS is as a framework to ensure that children are ready for school by the end of the foundation year. In many ways, this has the potential for educators to be influenced by a top-down effect where the early learning goals drive the content of the curriculum provision rather than being led by a child's level of development.

Although closely linked, the EYFS (DfE, 2021) separates literacy from language and communication, and rather than taking a plural approach to 'literacies' as discussed throughout this book, focuses on literacy as reading and writing and its role in comprehending and recreating texts. There is a particular emphasis on teaching children to read and write through a phonic approach as can be seen **in bold** in the following excerpt from the EYFS (DfE, 2021).

It is crucial for children to develop a life-long love of reading. Reading consists of two dimensions: language comprehension and word reading. Language comprehension (necessary for both reading and writing) starts from birth. It only develops when adults talk with children about the world around them and the books (stories and non-fiction) they read with them, and enjoy rhymes, poems and songs together. **Skilled word reading, taught later, involves both the speedy working out of the pronunciation of unfamiliar printed words (decoding) and the speedy recognition of familiar printed words**. Writing involves transcription (spelling and handwriting) and composition (articulating ideas and structuring them in speech, before writing).

This emphasis may mean that informed practitioners, who understand the many different considerations and approaches that need to be made in learning to read and write (see Chapters 4 and 5), have reduced opportunities to make their own decisions in favour of a narrow phonic approach. This potentially narrows their ability to make decisions about how to meet a wide range of different children's needs in literacy.

The three Early Learning Goals (ELGs) for literacy that children at the expected level of development should demonstrate are:

Comprehension

- Demonstrate understanding of what has been read to them by retelling stories and narratives using their own words and recently introduced vocabulary;
- Anticipate – where appropriate – key events in stories;
- Use and understand recently introduced vocabulary during discussions about stories, non-fiction, rhymes and poems and during role play.

Word reading

- Say a sound for each letter in the alphabet and at least 10 digraphs;
- Read words consistent with their phonic knowledge by sound-blending;
- Read aloud simple sentences and books that are consistent with their phonic knowledge, including some common exception words.

Writing

- Write recognisable letters, most of which are correctly formed;
- Spell words by identifying sounds in them and representing the sounds with a letter or letters;
- Write simple phrases and sentences that can be read by others.

This developmental approach to the curriculum, with an emphasis on preparing children to meet these early learning goals so that they are ready for school by the end of the foundation stage, is contentious. Some feel that these are too ambitious, particularly for summer-born children. A focus on ensuring that children meet these by the age of five has the potential for labelling those who don't meet them as failing. Any curriculum with 'goals' as part of it's framework that are reported nationally, potentially steers pedagogy from afar (Roberts-Holmes, 2014). Although very different from the English framework, the New Zealand Te Whāriki curriculum has similar issues in being a fixed framework for all children, and this will be considered next.

Alternative curricular approaches to literacy play: Te Whāriki

Written in both Māori and English, Te Whāriki, the Early Childhood Curriculum of New Zealand (Ministry of Education, 2017), is founded on the bi-cultural values that reflect both contemporary New Zealand and traditional Māori language and beliefs. The description, Te Whāriki, or woven flax mat, is used as a metaphor to demonstrate the interweaving of principles and strands necessary for learning from birth to six years old. Woven mats have symbolic and spiritual meaning in Māori culture and these meanings have been adopted to represent the cultural investment in early childhood,

> Weaving a whāriki takes knowledge, skill and time. It is almost always done collaboratively. When finished, an intricately woven whāriki is a taonga (prized object) valued for its artistry and kaupapa (initiative). (Ministry of Education, New Zealand, 2017, p. 10)

The Whāriki, as a symbol of early childhood learning, is created as a collaboration between the child, their parents/carers and whānau (family group), as well as the wider community. The structure of the weaving involves four broad curriculum principles: empowerment, holistic development, family and community, and relationships. These are interwoven with five curriculum strands: wellbeing, belonging, contribution, communication and exploration. The Kaiako (educator) has an important role for overseeing the weaving together of the principles and strands as young children move through their early education. Importantly, children are placed within the weaving as capable and competent learners, framed through the lens of their historical past and the cultural status that this provides.

> From lines that stretch back to the beginning of time, children are important living links between past, present and future, and a reflection of their ancestors. (Ministry of Education, New Zealand, 2017, p. 12)

Each child's course of learning will be formed differently dependent on their unique cultural environment and their growth within it. Te Whāriki does not have stages with structured next steps, but recognises learning as a complex inter-weaving of experiences and developments (Mutch and Trim, 2013). As Carr and May, the original coordinators of Te Whāriki write, it is a 'model of knowledge and understanding for young children as a tapestry of increasing complexity and richness. The weaving model of learning, conceptualises the child's development as a series of increasingly intricate patterns of linked experience and meaning, centred on cultural and individual purpose' (1996, p. 102).

By incorporating the multicultural beliefs, values and attitudes of children, their families, and members of the wider communities, Te Whāriki recognises learning as culturally situated. In alignment with this, learning to be literate is understood to be socially and culturally constructed, an essentially social practice where meanings and understandings are created in everyday encounters with others (see Vygotsky's language development theory in Chapter 2). Young chil-dren's literacy learning is, therefore, directed towards localised everyday prac-tices (Street, 2001), shifting the understanding of the literacy 'expert' away from the educational setting, towards the community, and prioritising the wealth of literacy experiences that each child and their family bring with them into the early childhood setting. According to guidance, early years educators should be 'actively supporting dual and multi-lingual literacy conventions and practices', 'valuing parent and whānau views and expectations on literacy' and 'curious about the social and literacy practices children enjoy outside their service, using these as a jumping off point for planning literacy experiences and activities' (Ministry of Education, New Zealand, n.d. para.3).

Kaiako (educators) must ensure that there is a commitment to recognis-ing Māori language – stories, symbols, arts and crafts, and as children move through their early learning journey, that the language or languages they experi-ence become more varied. Oral culture is viewed as the foundation of literacy learning, and consequently talk and conversation are prioritised in early educa-tors' practices with young children from infancy. This is part of a multiliteracy approach that supports children to connect wider cultural stories – oral, visual or written – to their own lives, alongside exploration of digital texts. Literacy goals are woven throughout the strands of Te Whāriki, but are predominantly in the Communication strand. The intention of these goals is that children experi-ence an environment where they develop non-verbal communication skills for a range of purposes, develop verbal communication skills for a range of purposes, experience the stories and symbols of their own and other cultures and discover and develop different ways to be creative and expressive (Ministry of Education, New Zealand, 2009).

The socio-cultural framework of Te Whāriki recognises early literacy learn-ing as an active experience that draws together children, materials and events.

Play is valued as a process of drawing or weaving together culture and materials within child-centred learning, and educators have a responsibility for facilitating quality play experiences where perspectives and contributions of children and their whanau (their extended family or community who live in the same area) are encouraged (Ministry of Education, New Zealand, 2017). Sharing the intentional connections that exist in children's play is communicated with parents and Whānau through learning stories (Nicolson and Bracefield, 2019).

Assessment of children's learning is through 'learning stories', a narrative genre (including written texts and photographs) that are uniquely fashioned for each child by interweaving personal experience into a textual format. Learning stories are commonly focused on a specific incident or episode, documenting what an educator (or parent) has seen a child (or group of children) doing. They are also sometimes as a result of children initiating interactions with teachers about events that are significant to them and their learning (Reese et al., 2019). It is common for the educator to match the strands of Te Whāriki to the story to try to explain what the child (or group of children) have learnt; however, learning stories are intended to highlight what the child can do, and is doing, rather than what they can't do. These learning stories are collected into a child's 'portfolio' and shared with families in order to create a dialogue between the early years setting and the child's home and community.

Reflection

Why are narrative stories a good way of capturing literacy learning? What 'tools' would you use to capture literacy learning as a story to share with others, e.g. photographs, video, etc.?

The multicultural strengths of the New Zealand early childhood curriculum are widely celebrated; however, tensions have been identified that are common in other similar child-centred curriculum frameworks. The problem lies in the conflict between Te Whāriki's broad approach where children's cultural and individual needs are foregrounded and the prescribed sequence of learning (see literacy goals) that is mapped out for all children. The guidance makes it clear that this sequence of learning is relatively flexible; however, the individual child cannot be the sole source of curriculum development, as is stated clearly within the documentation of Te Whāriki if there is a fixed framework, even one which attends to learner-centred experiences (Soler and Miller, 2003). Questions have also been raised about how literacy knowledge itself is characterised in Te Whāriki. McLachlan and Arrow (2015) argue that in emphasising the environment in learning diverse literacies (as a situated everyday practice), Te Whāriki is ignoring wider universal literacy practices that young children need to know in order to participate fully in society. This leads to literacy disparities between different groups of children, particularly disadvantaging those from an indigenous background. This argument, however, is predicated on ethnocentric assumptions where the authors have applied their own cultural assumptions about the value of literacy and what needs to be 'known', rather than considering the diversity inherent in literacies where value lies in cultural meaning making between the child, their families and their communities.

Alternative curricular approaches to literacy and play: Reggio Emilia

The preschools and infant and toddler centres of Reggio Emilia, a municipality in Italy, have become the centre of an influential world-wide approach to early years education driven by an image of the child as strong and powerful. Reggio Emilia is an extremely optimistic approach based on the notion that the child has extraordinary potential; each child is therefore a gifted child, and each adult working with them needs to match their curiosity, resourcefulness and adventurousness in order to be the gifted educators that young children deserve (Malaguzzi cited in Moss, 2004).

This way of conceptualising young children as intelligent, and with ambitious desires and requests for themselves (Malaguzzi, 1994), challenges assumptions that children are weak and/or incomplete and so need a universal framework that helps them to 'completion'. The philosophy that underpins Reggio Emilia rejects a curriculum that is future outcome orientated, with measurable steps showing 'progress', and instead provides an alternative model that emerges from the rich knowledge, skills, and competence that each baby, toddler and young child holds. In order to enact this emergent curriculum, a pedagogy of listening and dialogue with children is promoted. Educators are required to enter into a 'process of transformation, where you lose absolutely the possibility of controlling the final result' (Rinaldi, 2005, p. 184); a revisioning of the 'traditional' role of the educator with knowledge who leads the child. In the Reggio Emilia approach, educators support young children's learning through democratic action, embracing Dewey's theory of play (2015 [1902]). This engagement brings deep connective meaning making between children, adults and their environment, harking back to the connective theories of play espoused by Froebel (Bruce, 2011) (see Chapter 1 to explore these links further).

Rather than considering early education as a pedagogy where children have learning needs that adults must support, Reggio Emilia advocates a pedagogy based on children's rights. Each child viewed as a rightful subject is supported by the United Nations Convention for the Rights of the Child (UNCRC) (UNICEF, 1989). Within the UNCRC's 54 connected articles, children have a right to an education (Article 28), rights to relax and play (Article 31) and a right to freedom of expression (Article 13). Loris Malaguzzi, one of the founders of the Reggio

Emilia approach, argued that children should have a right to the best teachers, a right to excellent early years environments (building and resources), and importantly a right to have time as this is necessary for each child to be 'authors of their own learning' (Malaguzzi, 1994, p. 55).

Deconstructing the child differently from being objects of adult demands (Rinaldi, 1993) means that the onus is placed on children to create their own cultures and express their own social agency with others. Participation as a central tenet of Reggio Emilia is based on plurality (a respect of diverse cultures and differing points of view). Encouraging children's participation as an educational strategy 'generates and informs the feelings and culture of solidarity, responsibility and inclusion, and produces change and new cultures' (Reggio Children, Values, n.d., para. 3).

Learning activity emerges from children's individual and shared interests, their ideas forming the basis for in-depth project-based learning that can last a few weeks or a whole year. The educators or teachers in Reggio Emilia, support the children in groups to research the topics they are interested in and select diverse modes and mediums to represent and demonstrate to others what they have learnt in their play. This encourages children to be active constructors, or primary protagonists in their learning, and the carefully designed and materially rich learning environments within Reggio Emilia schools, that often include an atelier (studio or workshop), are developed to encourage children to question, investigate and explore. Within these carefully cultivated environments, the child's meaning making is socially constructed through discussion, debate and even discord (Hewett, 2001); children's knowledge of literacy understood to be influenced by social, cultural and material factors. Literacy knowledge is also provisional in that it changes over time; a 'tangle of spaghetti' as Malaguzzi famously described it (Moss, 2004). This meaning-making process recognises that there are multiple ways that children know about the world, therefore, there are multiple ways of knowing about literacy.

Learning literacy as a process of co-construction places the relationships that young children have with others as central to meaning making (Dahlberg et al., 2013). Children's relationships with parents (as the first teacher), their teachers (as the second) and the environment (as the third) form the basis for literacy learning. According to Malaguzzi (1996), the multiple ways that children choose to express, and communicate their learning as different 'languages' (see the 100 languages of children in Chapter 1) should be equally respected and valued; there should be no hierarchy in the literacies that children select to represent their ideas. This means that cultural and linguistic diversity is embraced, corresponding with multiliteracies and multimodal approaches to literacy learning (see Chapter 2). Young children viewed as capable of literacy users from birth are supported to use their bodies and objects to symbolise their thoughts and feelings (Rubizzi and Bonlauri in Edwards et al., 2011). Tools and objects, skills in graphic arts are integrated into projects to support text-making production from a young age. Children are encouraged to understand the rules and purposes of literacy; how it is constructed and produced by deconstructing the elements in producing it.

Children's learning is made visible through a process of pedagogical documentation (Dahlberg et al., 2013). Like the Learning Stories within the Te Whāriki curriculum, documentation are the stories of children's learning; however, these visually presented stories are created through a rigorous process of research stimulated by questions and lines of enquiry from the children and the teachers. This process of documentation aligns to the democratic principles of the Reggio Emilia pedagogy, as there is a re-positioning of the teacher from an all-knowing arbitrator of learning focused on evidencing what literacy has been learnt, into one who follows the child's lead to find out how literacies have been learnt. It is this process of documenting learning, where a curriculum can be found, one that locates the learning steps for the child from which teachers and parents can plan resources and support.

Rinaldi (2005) refers to pedagogical documentation as visible listening, where traces of learning can be identified and shared with others. This requires a careful listening or attunement of adults to the ways that children are learning. To do this well, teachers select a range of visual methods and graphic design processes to capture the thoughts, feelings, values and culture of the children with whom they work. Examples of pedagogical documentation reveal how literacies are learnt through movement across different spaces as children intra-act with different materials and the environment in their exploratory play. Children's knowledge represented within pedagogical documentation shows that it is not confined to specific areas of learning (e.g. maths, literacy, art), but an amalgam of knowledges that are brought together within learning encounters. As pieces of 'research in progress', pedagogical documentation is often informally displayed and kept alive by being regularly amended, inviting intra-action with other teachers, children, their families, and famously the wider community through displays, publications and exhibitions (Reggio Children, Exhibitions, n.d.). Many representations of children's pedagogical documentation are beautifully rendered and published as a way of valuing and celebrating children's learning. To appreciate this fully, we recommend viewing examples published by Reggio Emilia nurseries and preschools, for example on the Reflections Nursery website https://reflectionsnurseries.co.uk/

Planning for rich literacies

Now think back to the vignette at the beginning of this chapter. Here are the reflections of an educator carefully observing Samuel, how he has organised objects to support a developing story and his re-enactment of the story. Consider how this adult might have further enhanced, supported, or indeed prevented further possible opportunities that could have extended opportunities for literacy play:

Case Study

Adult Observational Reflections

I observed Samuel in the sand. He caught my attention because he was on his own. I usually feel a bit uncomfortable when I see children playing by themselves, but I decided that because I was doing an observation that I would watch and wait to see what happened next. It was interesting to see that the lack of water in the tray did not bother him. I might have usually offered to top it up. I noticed that far from prohibiting play, it encouraged him to make marks because mark-making with the water was possible as a result of the plastic available around the edge of the tray. I noticed that he was making marks that looked similar to the letters in his name. Again, I might usually have helped him to form these correctly and even made suggestions about what other letters he could try to write. It was interesting that he then picked up the truck lying nearby and started 'driving' it on the paving stones, creating new marks. The tyres of the truck left some interesting marks and I think that this is what grabbed his attention. He made sounds as he took the truck on his imaginary journey. I wonder what the story was all about. I wonder if I should have intervened to suggest that we use some wood to create a bridge over the water to make some more interesting terrain for him to drive the truck through?

The EYFS states that, 'children learn by leading their own play and by taking part in play which is guided by adults' (DfE, 2021, p. 16). However, as you can see from the reflections above, the decision to intervene is based on the intention of the adult.

Reflective questions

How might the adults' interventions have changed if they had been working within each of these different frameworks:

> The EYFS?
> Te Whāriki?
> Reggio Emilia?

Considering your intentions in what to do next to support children's learning is an important aspect of practice. It isn't necessarily a case of letting either the child or adult lead the activity. It is more nuanced than this. There are subtleties of communication at work here. Your mere presence can stop a child's imagination in its tracks. Consider how often your attention has been thwarted by the imposition of others. To what extent does this 'ruin your train of thought'? How easily we can be distracted by the proximity of others. This isn't to say that we should never intervene or have a presence but that we need to be able to judge when and how this should take place. We also need to understand our reasons and motivations for doing so. These are shaped by the frameworks that guide our practice.

By examining these different early childhood curricular models we can see that there is no global agreement of what literacy is, or what literacies look like; however there are understandings that we can take forward in developing pedagogical practices to support literacies as vital components of children's play. Most models and frameworks emphasise that young children's languages are social and culturally derived and given encouragement and support can be expressed in multiple forms. Children's languages provide the foundation for symbolic text making (literacies). Literacies are, therefore, essentially plural and diverse, and the fluidity of play, its self-driven spontaneity as well as its democratic and participatory possibilities, provide a means to facilitate and amplify these multiliteracies.

What we can take from these pedagogical curriculum approaches is that educators need to find ways of listening with care and tuning into the multiple ways that young children play with literacies and follow the child's lead as a responsive play partner. Davies argues that listening to children in their play is an emergent process, describing it as 'listening to thought happening... to the intensities of forces working on and through us' (2014, p. 35). This is delicate and intricate work, that demands educators to note, map and document young children's literacies attentively. Doing this well will invite others to hear and see the inventiveness and transformational qualities that exist in children's literacy play and open up new ways of thinking about literacies for all engaged in young children's education.

In summary

- To ensure that the curriculum offers children rich learning opportunities, language and literacies should be developed through play.
- Practitioners need to examine their motivation for intervening in children's play to foster rather that inhibit children's language and emerging literacies.
- Different curricular models provide us with more insight into how different types of literacy can be supported in diverse ways.
- Educators need to find ways to listen carefully and represent children's play through varied documentation methods that acknowledge the rich and diverse literacies of children.

Having read this chapter, here are some **discussion questions** to help you in using your curriculum documentation to plan for literacy play provision:

1. How do you 'listen' to children's learning? List all of the different ways.
2. What is your understanding of 'pedagogical documentation' and 'learning stories' and how they support learning and assessment? How can you ensure that assessment of children's literacy learning is 'useful'?
3. How do you share your thinking about practice with colleagues, parents and the wider community to benefit children's learning? Where are the reflective spaces for you to ask yourself 'why?'

Further recommended reading

This book will challenge your thinking about some of the more accepted ways of thinking about practice and help you to consider alternative pedagogical approaches.

Birth to Five Matters (2021) *Birth to Five Matters*. Available online: www.birthto5matters.org.uk/ (Accessed 09.04.21).

Moss, P. (2018) *Alternative Narratives in Early Childhood*. Abingdon, Oxon: Routledge.

Comprehensive non-statutory guidance written 'by the sector for the sector' to support practitioners in all areas of the Early Years Foundation Stage. We particularly recommend the extensive resources available on this website to support young children's literacies.

REFERENCES

Arizpe, E. (2014) Wordless picturebooks: Critical and educational perspectives on meaning-making. In B. Kummerling-Meibauer (Ed.), *Picturebooks. Representation and Narration* (pp. 91–106). New York and London: Routledge.

Arnott, L., Palaiologou, I. and Gray, C. (2019) An ecological exploration of the internet of toys in early childhood everyday life. In G. Mascheroni and D. Holloway (Eds.), *The Internet of Toys: Practices, Affordances and the Political Economy of Children's Play* (pp. 135–157). Cham, Switzerland: Palgrave Macmillan.

Baird, A., Laugharne, J., Maagerø, E. and Tønnesse, E. (2015) *Child readers and the worlds of the picture book. Children's Literature in Education, 47*, 1–17. DOI: 10.1007/s10583-015-9244-4.

Bar-Haim, S. (2017) The liberal playground: Susan Isaacs, psychoanalysis and progressive education in the interwar era. *History of the Human Sciences*, 30 (1), 94–117. DOI:10.1177/0952695116668123.

Barad. K. (2007) *Meeting the Universe Halfway: Quantum Physics and the Entanglement of Matter and Meaning.* London: Duke University Press.

Bateman, A. (2018) Ventriloquism as early literacy practice: Making meaning in pretend play. *Early Years*, 38 (1), 68–85. DOI: 10.1080/09575146.2016.1254162.

Bennett, J. (2010) *Vibrant Matter: A Political Ecology of Things.* London: Duke University Press.

Bilton, H. (2010) *Outdoor Learning in the Early Years* (3rd ed.). London: Routledge.

Bilton, H. (2020) Values stop play? Teachers' attitudes to the early years outdoor environment. *Early Child Development and Care*, 190 (1), 12–20. DOI: 10.1080/03004430.2019.1653548.

Bodrova, E. and Leong, J. (2003) The importance of being playful. *Educational Leadership*, 60 (7), 50–53.

Bodrova, E. and Leong, D. J. (2015) Vygotskian and post-Vygotskian views of children's play. *American Journal of Play*, 7 (3), 371–388.

BookTrust (n.d.) *Bookstart.* Available online: www.booktrust.org.uk/what-we-do/programmes-and-campaigns/bookstart/ (Accessed 20.4.21).

Braidotti, R. (2017) *Posthuman, all too human: the memoirs and aspirations of a posthumanist. The 2017 Tanner Lectures.* Yale University. Available online: tannerlectures.utah.edu/Manuscript%20for%20Tanners%20Foundation%20Final%20Oct%201.pdf (Accessed 20.4.21).

Brandt, A., Gebrian, M. and Slevc, R. L. (2012) Music and early language acquisition. *Frontiers in Psychology*, 3, 1–7.

Brooker, L. (2002) *Starting School: Young Children Learning Cultures*. London: McGraw-Hill Education.

Broom, C. (2017) Exploring the relations between childhood experiences in nature and young adults' environmental attitudes and behaviours. *Australian Journal of Environmental Education*, 33 (1), 34–47. DOI: 10.1017/aee.2017.1.

Bruce, T. (2011) *Learning Through Play: For Babies, Toddlers and Young Children*. London: Hodder Education.

Bruce. T. (2012) The whole child. In T. Bruce, *Early Childhood Practice: Froebel Today*. London: Sage.

Bruce, T. (2015) *Early Childhood Education* (3rd ed.). London: Hodder Arnold.

Bruce, T., McNair, L. and Whinnet, J. (Eds.) (2020) *Putting Storytelling at the Heart of Early Childhood Practice: A Reflective Guide for Early Years Practitioners*. Abingdon, Oxon: Routledge.

Brühlmeier, A. (2010) *Head, Heart and Hand. Education in the Spirit of Pestalozzi*. Cambridge: Sophia Books.

Bruner, J. S. (1966) *Toward a Theory of Instruction*. Cambridge, MA: Belkapp Press.

Bruner, J. S. (1978) The role of dialogue in language acquisition. In A. Sinclair, R. J. Jarvelle and W. J. M. Levelt (Eds.), *The Child's Concept of Language*. New York: Springer-Verlag.

Bruner, J. S. (1986) *Actual Minds, Possible Worlds*. Cambridge, MA: Harvard University Press.

Bruner, J. S. (1991) The narrative construction of reality. *Critical Inquiry*, 18, 1–21.

Bruner, J. S. (1992) The narrative construction of reality. In H. Beilin and P. B. Pufall (Eds.), *The Jean Piaget Symposium Series. Piaget's Theory: Prospects and Possibilities* (pp. 229–248). New Jersey: Lawrence Erlbaum Associates, Inc.

Burke, R. and Duncan, J. (2015) *Bodies as Sites of Cultural Reflection in Early Childhood Education*. Abingdon, Oxon: Routledge.

Burman, E. (2008) *Deconstructing Developmental Psychology* (2nd ed.). Hove: Routledge/Taylor and Francis.

Burnett, C., Merchant, G., Pahl, K. and Rowsell, J. (2014) The (im)materiality of literacy: The significance of subjectivity to new literacies research. *Discourse: Studies in the Cultural Politics of Education*, 35 (1), 90–103. DOI: 10.1080/01596306.2012.739469.

Canfield, F., Seery, A., Weisleder, A., Workman, C., Brockmeyer, C., Roby, C. E., Payne, R., Levine, S., Mogilner, L., Dreyer, B. and Mendelsohn, A. (2020) Encouraging parent–child book sharing: Potential additive benefits of literacy promotion in health care and the community. *Early Childhood Research Quarterly*, 50 (1), 221–229. DOI: 10.1016/j.ecresq.2018.11.002.

Cannella, G. S. and Viruru, R. (2004) *Childhood and Postcolonization: Power, Education, and Contemporary Practice*. New York: Routledge.

Carr, M. and May, H. (1996) Te Whāriki, making a difference for the under-fives? *The new National Early Childhood Curriculum. Delta*, 48 (1), 101–112.

Carruthers, E. and Worthington, M. (2006) *Children's Mathematics: Making Marks, Making Meaning* (2nd ed.). London: Sage.

Cekaite, A. and Björk-Willén, P. (2018) Enchantment in storytelling: Co-operation and participation in children's aesthetic experience. *Linguistics and Education*, 48, 52–60. DOI: 10.1016/j.linged.2018.08.005.

Chaudron, S., Plowman, L., Beutel, M. E., Cernikova, M., Donoso Navarette., V., Dreier, M., Fletcher-Watson, B., Heikkilä, A. S., Kontríková, V., Korkeamäki, R. L., Livingstone, S., Marsh, J., Mascheroni, G., Micheli, M., Milesi, D., Müller, K. W., Myllylä-Nygård, T., Niska, M., Olkina, O., Ottovordemgentschenfelde S., Ribbens, W., Richardson, J., Schaack, C., Shlyapnikov, V., Smahel, D., Soldatova, G. and Wölfling, K. (2015) *Young Children (0–8) and Digital Technology – EU report.* Luxembourg: Publications Office of the European Union.

Chomsky, N. (1965) *Aspects of the Theory of Syntax.* Cambridge, MA: MIT Press.

Chomsky, N. (1986) *Knowledge of Language: Its Nature, Origin and Use.* New York: Praeger.

Christie, J. and Roskos, K. (2013) Play's potential in early literacy development. *In Encyclopedia on Early Childhood Development.* Available online: www.child-encyclopedia.com/play/according-experts/plays-potential-early-literacy-development (Accessed 10.04.21).

Clark, M. (2013) Research evidence on the first phonics check for all Year 1 children in England: Is it accurate and is it necessary? *Education Journal*, 168, 12–15.

Clark. M (2014) *Learning to be Literate: Insights from Policy to Practice.* Birmingham: Greendale Education.

Clay, M. (1975) *What did I Write?* Oxford: Heinemann Educational Books.

Clay, M. M. (1985) *The Early Detection of Reading Difficulties* (3rd ed.). Auckland, NZ: Heinemann.

CLPE (Centre for Literacy in Primary Education) (n.d.) *Developing Ideas through Role Play.* Available online: clpe.org.uk/powerofpictures/creative-approaches/2 (Accessed 20.4.21).

Cope, B. and Kalantzis, M. (2000) *Multiliteracies: Literacy Learning and the Design of Social Futures.* London: Routledge.

Corbeil, M., Trehub, S. E. and Peretz, I. (2013) Speech vs. singing: Infants choose happier sounds. *Frontiers in Psychology*, 4 (372), 1–11.

Corbeil, M., Trehub, S. E. and Peretz, I. (2016) Singing delays the onset of infant distress. *Infancy*, 21 (3), 373–391.

Corsaro, W. A. (2003) *We're Friends, Right?: Inside Kids' Culture.* Washington, D.C.: Joseph Henry Press.

Cowan, K. (2019) Digital meaning making: Reggio Emilia-inspired practice in Swedish preschools. *Media Education Research Journal*, 8 (2), 11–29. DOI: 10.1177/14687984030031003.

Cowley. S. (2019) *The Ultimate Guide to Mark Making in the Early Years*. London: Featherstone, Bloomsbury.

Cremin, T. and Myhill, D. (2012) *Writing Voices: Creating Communities of Writers*. Abingdon, Oxon: Routledge.

Cremin, Y., Chappell, K. and Craft, A. (2013) Reciprocity between narrative, questioning and imagination in the early and primary years: Examining the role of narrative in possibility thinking. *Thinking Skills and Creativity*, 9, 135–151.

Cremin, T., Flewitt R., Mardell, B. and Swann, J. (2017) Introduction. In T. Cremin, R. Flewitt, B. Mardell and J. Swann (Eds.), *Storytelling in Early Childhood: Enriching Language, Literacy and Classroom Culture*. Abingdon, Oxon: Routledge.

Dahlberg, G. and Moss, P. (2005) *Ethics and Politics in Early Childhood Education*. Abingdon, Oxon: RoutledgeFalmer.

Dahlberg, G., Moss, P. and Pence, A. (2013) *Beyond Quality in Early Childhood Education and Care: Languages of Evaluation* (3rd ed.). Abingdon, Oxon: Routledge.

Daniels, K., Bower, K., Burnett, C., Escott, H., Hatton, A., Ehiyazaryan-White, E. and Monkhouse, J. (2020) Early years teachers and digital literacies: Navigating a kaleidoscope of discourses. *Education and Information Technologies*, 25, 2415–2426. DOI: 10.1007/s10639-019-10047-9.

Davies, B. (2014) *Listening to Children: Being and Becoming*. Routledge: Abingdon

Deleuze, G. and Guattari, F. (2004) *A Thousand Plateaus: Capitalism and Schizophrenia* (Trans. B. Massumi). London: Continuum.

Devi, A., Fleer, M. and Li, L. (2018) 'We set up a small world': Preschool teachers' involvement in children's imaginative play. *International Journal of Early Years Education*, 26 (3), 295–311. DOI:10.1080/09669760.2018.1452720.

Dewey, J. (1910) *How we Think*. Boston, MA: D.C. Heath & Co.

Dewey, J. (2015 [1902]) *The Child and the Curriculum*. Whitefish, MT: Literary Licensing, LLC.

DfE (Department for Education) (2021) *Statutory Framework for the Early Years Foundation Stage*. DfE Available online: assets.publishing.service.gov.uk/government/uploads/system/uploads/attachment_data/file/974907/EYFS_framework_-_March_2021.pdf (Accessed 20.4.21).

Dissanayake, E. (2000) *Art and Intimacy: How the Arts Began*. London: University of Washington Press.

Dombey, H. (2013) *Teaching Writing: What the Evidence Says: UKLA Argues for an Evidence-informed Approach to Teaching and Testing Young Children's Writing*. Leicester: UKLA.

Durst, A. (2010) *Women Educators in the Progressive Era: The Women Behind Dewey's Laboratory School*. London: Palgrave.

Dyson, A. H. (1993) From prop to mediator: The changing role of written language in children's symbolic repertoires. In B. Spodek and O. N. Saracho (Eds.), *Yearbook in Early Childhood Education: Language and Literacy in Early Childhood Education* (Vol. 4, pp. 21–41). New York: Teachers College Press.

Edwards, C., Gandini, L., Forman, G. and Reggio, C. S. (Eds.) (2011) *The Hundred Languages of Children: The Reggio Emilia Experience in Transformation* (3rd ed.). CA.: ABC-CLIO.

Edwards, S. (2013) Digital play in the early years: A contextual response to the problem of integrating technologies and play-based pedagogies in the early childhood curriculum. *European Early Childhood Education Research Journal*, 21 (2), 199–212. DOI: 10.1080/1350293X.2013.789190.

Edwards, S. (2018) Play-based Learning: Digital play. In Centre of Excellence for Early Childhood Development, *Encyclopedia on Early Childhood Development*, 1–6. Available online: www.child-encyclopedia.com/sites/default/files/textes-experts/en/4978/digital-play.pdf (Accessed 20.4.21).

Edwards, S. and Bird, J. (2017) Observing and assessing young children's digital play in the early years: Using the Digital Play Framework. *Journal of Early Childhood Research*, 15 (2), 158–173. DOI: 10.1177/1476718X15579746.

EEF (Education Endowment Foundation) (2017) *Early Years Toolkit*. Available online: educationendowmentfoundation.org.uk/evidence-summaries/early-years-toolkit/ (Accessed 20.4.21).

EEF (Education Endowment Foundation) (2018a) *The Attainment Gap*. Available online: educationendowmentfoundation.org.uk/public/files/Annual_Reports/EEF_Attainment_Gap_Report_2018.pdf (Accessed 10.4.21).

EEF (Education Endowment Foundation) (2018b) *Preparing for Literacy – Improving communication, language and literacy in the early years: Guidance report*. Available online: educationendowmentfoundation.org.uk/public/files/Publications/Literacy/Preparing_Literacy_Guidance_2018.pdf (Accessed 10.04.21).

Egan, K. (1986) *Teaching as Storytelling*. London, Canada: The Althouse Press.

Else, P. (2009) *The Value of Play*. London: Continuum International Publishing Group.

Engel, S. (2005) The narrative worlds of what-is and what-if. *Cognitive Development*, 20 (4), 514–525.

Erstad, O. and Gillen, J. (2019) Theorizing digital literacy practices in early childhood. In O. Erstad, R. Flewitt, B. Kümmerling-Meibauer and Í. Pereira (Eds.), *The Routledge Handbook of Digital Literacies in Early Childhood* (pp. 31–44). Abingdon, Oxon: Routledge.

Evans, J. (2012) 'This is Me': Developing literacy and a sense of self through play, talk and stories. *Education 3–13*, 40 (3), 315–331. DOI: 10.1080/03004279.2010.531038.

Evans, V. (2014) *The Language Myth: Why Language is not an Instinct*. Cambridge: Cambridge University Press.

Fatherhood Institute (2010) *Booktrust Family Reading Activity Survey – Summary Report*. Available Online: www.booktrust.org.uk/globalassets/resources/research/fatherhood-institute-survey-sept-2010-exec-summary.pdf (Accessed 20.04.21).

Fernald, A., Taeschner, T., Dunn, J., Papousek, M., De Boysson-Bardies, B. and Fukui, I. (1989) A cross-language study of prosodic modifications in mothers' and fathers' speech to preverbal infants. *Journal of Child Language*, 16 (3), 477–501.

Fisher, J. (2016) *Interacting or Interfering? Improving Interactions in The Early Years.* Maidenhead: Open University Press.

Fisher, R., Jones, S. and Larking, S. (2010) *Using Talk to Support Writing.* London: Sage.

Fleer, M. (2018a) Conceptual playworlds: The role of imagination in play and learning. *Early Years*. DOI: 10.1080/09575146.2018.1549024.

Fleer, M. (2018b) Digital animation: New conditions for children's development in play-based setting. *British Journal Educational Technology*, 49, 943–958. DOI: 10.1111/bjet.12637.

Flewitt, R. (2005) Is every child's voice heard? Researching the different ways 3-year-old children communicate and make meaning at home and in a pre-school playgroup. *Early Years*, 25 (3), 207–222. DOI: 10.1080/09575140500251558

Flewitt, R. (2006) Using video to investigate preschool classroom interaction: Education research assumptions and methodological practices. *Visual Communication*, 5 (1), 25–50. DOI:10.1177/1470357206060917

Flewitt, R. (2013) *TACTYC Occasional Paper 3: Early Literacy: A broader vision.* Available online: http://eprints.ncrm.ac.uk/3132/1/flewitt_occasional-paper3.pdf (Accessed 10.4.21).

Flewitt, R. (2017) Equity and diversity through story. In T. Cremin, R. Flewitt, B. Mardell and J. Swann (Eds.), *Storytelling in Early Childhood: Enriching Language, Literacy and Classroom Culture* (pp. 150–168). Abingdon, Oxon: Routledge.

Flewitt, R., Messer, D. and Kucirkova, N. (2015) New directions for early literacy in a digital age: The iPad. *Journal of Early Childhood Literacy*, 15 (3), 289–310. DOI: doi.org/10.1177/1468798414533560.

Flynn, E. (2018) Storying experience: Young children's early use of story genres. *Text & Talk*, 38 (4), 457–480. DOI: 10.1515/text-2018-0010.

Fotakopoulou, O., Hatzigianni, M., Dardanou, M., Unstad, T. and O'Connor, J. (2020) A cross-cultural exploration of early childhood educators' beliefs and experiences around the use of touchscreen technologies with children under 3 years of age. *European Early Childhood Education Research Journal*, 28 (2), 272–285. DOI: 10.1080/1350293X.2020.1735744.

Froebel, F. (1826, trans. 1912) *Froebel's Chief Writings on Education* (Trans. S. S. F. Fletcher and J. Welton). London: Edward Arnold.

Froebel, F. (1887) *The Education of Man* (Trans. W. N. Hailmann). London: D. Appleton Century.

Froebel Trust (2019) *Froebelian Principles.* Available online: www.froebel.org.uk/about-us/froebelian-principles (Accessed 20.4.21).

Furedi, F. (2008) *Paranoid Parenting.* London: Continuum.

González-Monteagudo, J. (2011) Jerome Bruner and the challenges of the narrative turn: Then and now. *Journal of Narrative Inquiry*, 21, 295–302. DOI:10.1075/ni.21.2.07gon.

Goodman, K. (2005) *What's Whole in Whole Language* (20th annual ed.). Berkeley, CA: RDR.

Goouch, K. and Powell, S. (2013) *The Baby Room: Principles, Policy and Practice*. Maidenhead: Open University Press.

Goswami, U. (2010) Language, music and children's brains: A rhythmic timing perspective on language and music as cognitive systems. In P. Rebuschat et al. (Eds.), *Language and Music as Cognitive Systems* (pp. 292–301). Oxford: Oxford University Press.

Grieshaber, S. and McArdle, F. (2010) *The Trouble with Play*. Maidenhead: Oxford University Press.

Griffiths, N. (2001) *Once Upon a Time… Literacy Today*, 26, 9.

Gupta, A. (2009) Vygotskian perspectives on using dramatic play to enhance children's development and balance creativity with structure in the early childhood classroom. *Early Child Development and Care*, 179 (8), 1041–1054. DOI:10.1080/03004430701731654.

Hall, E. (2009) Mixed messages: The role and value of drawing in early education. *International Journal of Early Years Education*, 17 (3), 179–190. DOI: 10.1080/09669760903424507.

Hall, N. and Robinson, A. (2003) *Exploring Writing and Play in the Early Years* (2nd ed.). London: David Fulton.

Halliday, M. A. K. (1978) *Language as Social Semiotic: The Social Interpretation of Language and Meaning*. London: Edward Arnold.

Harwood, D. R. and Collier, D. (2017) The matter of the stick. *Journal of Early Childhood Literacy*, 17 (3), 336–352. DOI: 10.1177/1468798417712340.

Hernwall, P. (2016) 'We have to be professional' – Swedish preschool teachers' conceptualisation of digital media. *Nordic Journal of Digital Literacy*, 11 (1), 5–23. DOI: 10.18261/issn.1891-943x-2016-01-01.

Hewett, V. M. (2001) Examining the Reggio Emilia approach to early childhood education. *Early Childhood Education Journal*, 29, 95–100. DOI: 10.1023/A:1012520828095.

Howard, J. (2002) Eliciting young children's perceptions of play, work and learning using the activity apperception story procedure. *Early Child Development and Care*, 172 (5), 489–502. DOI: 10.1080/03004430214548.

Howard, J. (2018) Play and development in the young child. In S. Powell and K. Smith (Eds.), *An Introduction to Early Childhood* (pp. 103–113). London: Sage.

Howard, J., Jenvey, V. and Hill, C. (2006) Children's categorisation of play and learning based on social context. *Early Child Development and Care*, 176 (3–4), 379–393. DOI: 10.1080/03004430500063804.

Howe, S. (2016) What play means to us: Exploring children's perspectives on play in an English Year 1 classroom. *European Early Childhood Education Research Journal*, 24 (5), 748–759. DOI: 10.1080/1350293X.2016.1213567b.

Hutchinson, J., Bonetti, S., Crenna-Jennings, W. and Akhal, A. (2019) *Education in England: Annual Report 2019*. Education Policy Institute. Available online: epi.org.uk/wp-content/uploads/2019/07/EPI-Annual-Report-2019.pdf (Accessed 16.06.21).

Hutt, C. (1979) Play in the under 5s: Form, development and function. In J. G. Howell (Ed.), *Modern Perspectives in the Psychiatry of Infancy* (pp. 94–141). The Hague: Bruner/Maazel.

Imray, S. and Clements, K. (2020) Someone killed Goldilocks and they didn't live happily ever after..." Isabella age 3 years: How regular storytelling helps to develop creativity and narrative role play. In T. Bruce, L. McNair and J. Whinnet (Eds.), *Putting Storytelling at the Heart of Early Childhood Practice: A Reflective Guide for Early Years Practitioners* (pp. 15–30). Abingdon, Oxon: Routledge.

Ingold, T. (2007) *Lines: A Brief History*. Abingdon, Oxon: Routledge.

Ingold, T. (2011) *Being Alive: Essays on Movement, Knowledge and Description*. Abingdon, Oxon: Routledge.

Isaacs, S. (1951) *Social Development in Young Children*. London: Routledge.

Jackson, A. and Mazzei, L. (2013) Plugging one text into another: Thinking with theory in qualitative research. *Qualitative Inquiry,* 19 (4), 261–271. DOI:10.1177/1077800412471510.

James, K. H. (2010) Sensori-motor experience leads to changes in visual processing in the developing brain. *Developmental Science*, 13, 279–88.

Jarvis, P. (2007) Dangerous activities within an invisible playground: A study of emergent male football play and teachers' perspectives of outdoor free play in the early years of primary school. *International Journal of Early Years Education*, 15 (3), 245–259. DOI: 10.1080/09669760701516918.

Jarvis, P. (2013) *TACTYC Reflections Paper: The McMillan Sisters and the 'Deptford Welfare Experiment'*. Available online: tactyc.org.uk/wp-content/uploads/2013/11/Reflection-Jarvis.pdf (Accessed 09.04.21).

Jewitt, C. (2011) Different approaches to multimodality. In C. Jewitt (Ed.), *The Routledge Handbook of Multimodal Analysis* (pp. 28–39). Abingdon, Oxon: Routledge.

Johnston, R. and Watson, J. (2005) *The Effects of Synthetic Phonics Teaching on Reading and Spelling Attainment: A Seven Year Longitudinal Study*. Scottish Executive Education Department. Available online: dera.ioe.ac.uk/14793/1/0023582.pdf (Accessed 20.04.21).

Jolley, R. P. (2010) *Children and Pictures*. Chichester: Wiley-Blackwell.

Juelskjaer, M. and Schwennesen, N. (2012) Intra-active entanglements – An interview with Karen Barad. *Kvinder, Kon and Forskning*, 1 (2), 10–24. Available online: www.researchgate.net/publication/267863856_Intra-active_entanglements_an_interview_with_Karen_Barad (Accessed 20.4.21).

Kalantzis, M. and Cope, B. (2008) Language education and multiliteracies. In S. May and H. Hornberger (Eds.), *Encyclopedia of Language and Education* (pp. 195–211). New York: Springer.

Kenney, C. K. (2016) Focus on family: It's ok to play: The importance of playing while reading aloud to young children. *Childhood Education*, 92 (2), 161–163. DOI: 10.1080/00094056.2016.1150760.

Kewalramani, S., Palaiologou, I., Arnott, L. and Dardanou, M. (2020) The integration of the internet of toys in early childhood education: A platform for multi-layered interactions. *European Early Childhood Education Research Journal*, 28 (2), 197–213. DOI: 10.1080/1350293X.2020.1735738.

Kingdon, Z. (2020) Play as role-play: A Vygotskian analysis. In Z. Kingdon (Ed.), *A Vygotskian Analysis of Children's Play Behaviours: Beyond the Home Corner.* Abingdon, Oxon: Routledge.

Kress, G. (2000) *Early Spelling: Between Convention and Creativity.* Abingdon, Oxon: Routledge.

Kress, G. (2003) *Literacy in the New Media Age.* Abingdon, Oxon: Routledge.

Kress, G. (2010) *Multimodality: A Social Semiotic Approach to Contemporary Communication.* Abingdon, Oxon: Routledge.

Kress, G. and Van Leeuwen, T. (2001) *Multimodal Discourse: The Modes and Media of Contemporary Communication.* London: Arnold Publishers.

Kress, G. and Van Leeuwen, T. (2006) *Reading Images: The Grammar of Visual Design* (2nd ed.). Abingdon, Oxon: Routledge.

Kuby, C., Rucker, T. and Kirchhofer, J. (2015) 'Go be a writer': Intra-activity with materials, time and space in literacy learning. *Journal of Early Childhood Literacy*, 15 (3), 394–419. DOI: 10.1177/1468798414566702.

Kucirkova, N., Littleton, K. and Cremin, T. (2017) Young children's reading for pleasure with digital books: Six key facets of engagement. *Cambridge Journal of Education*, 47 (1), 67–84. DOI: 10.1080/0305764X.2015.1118441.

Kucirkova, N., Messer, D., Sheehy, K. and Flewitt, R. (2013) Sharing personalised stories on iPads: A close look at one parent–child interaction. *Literacy*, 47, 115–122. DOI: 10.1111/lit.12003.

Lancaster, L. (2007) Representing the ways of the world: How children under three start to use syntax in graphic signs. *Journal of Early Childhood Literacy*, 7 (2), 123–154. DOI: 10.1177/1468798407079284.

Lee, T. (2016) *Princesses, Dragons and Helicopter Stories: Storytelling and Story Acting in the Early Years.* Abingdon, Oxon: Routledge.

Lenz-Taguchi, H. (2010) *Going Beyond the Theory/Practice Divide in Early Childhood Education.* Abingdon, Oxon: Routledge.

Lepage, J. and Théoret, H. (2007) The mirror neuron system: grasping others? Actions from birth? *Developmental Science*, 10 (5), 513–523.

Lieberman, N. (1977) *Playfulness: Its Relationship to Imagination and Creativity.* London: Educational Psychology.

Lindqvist G. (1995) *The Aesthetics of Play: A Didactic Study of Play and Culture in Preschools*. Uppsala, Sweden: Uppsala Studies in Education.

Lobman, C. (2003) What should we create today? Improvisational teaching in play-based classrooms. *Early Years*, 23 (2), 131–142. DOI: 10.1080/0957514 0303104.

Louv, R. (2005) *Last Child in the Woods*. London: Atlantic.

Luo, R. and Tamis-LeMonda, C. S. (2019) Preschool book-sharing and oral story-telling experiences in ethnically diverse, low-income families. *Early Child Development and Care*, 189 (10), 1602–1619. DOI: 10.1080/03004430.2017.1400542.

Malaguzzi, L. (1994) *Your Image of the Child: Where Teaching Begins*. Available Online: www.reggioalliance.org/downloads/malaguzzi:ccie:1994.pdf (Accessed 20.04.21).

Malaguzzi, L. (1996) *The Hundred Languages of Children: Narrative of the Possible. Catalogue of the Exhibit 'The Hundred Languages of Children'*. Reggio Emilia, Italy: Reggio Children.

Malloch, S. and Trevarthen, C. (2009) *Communicative Musicality: Exploring the Basis of Human Companionship*. Oxford: Oxford University Press.

Marsh, J. (2017) The internet of toys: A posthuman and multimodal analysis of connected play. *Teachers College Record*, 119 (12), 1–32.

Marsh, J. (2018) Childhood in the digital age. In S. Powell and K. Smith (Eds.), *An Introduction to Early Childhood Studies* (pp. 53–63). London: Sage.

Marsh, J., Murris, K., Ng'ambi, D., Parry, R., Scott, F., Thomsen, B. S., Bishop, J., Bannister, C., Dixon, K., Giorza, T., Peers, J., Titus, S., Da Silva, H., Doyle, G., Driscoll, A., Hall, L., Hetherington, A., Krönke, M., Margary, T., Morris, A., Nutbrown, B., Rashid, S., Santos, J., Scholey, E., Souza, L. and Woodgate, A. (2020) *Children, Technology and Play. Billund, Denmark: The LEGO Foundation*. Available online: www.legofoundation.com/media/2965/children-tech-and-play_full-report.pdf (Accessed 20.04.21).

Marsh, J., Plowman, L., Yamada-Rice, D., Bishop, J. C., Lahmar, J., Scott, F., Davenport, A., Davis, S., French, K., Piras, M., Thornhill, S., Robinson, P. and Winter, P. (2015) *Exploring Play and Creativity in Pre-Schoolers' Use of Apps – Final Project Report*. Available online: www.techandplay.org/reports/TAP_Final_Report. pdf (Accessed 26.10.21).

Marsh, J., Plowman, L., Yamada-Rice, D., Bishop, J. and Scott, F. (2016) Digital play: A new classification. *Early Years*, 36 (3), 242–253. DOI: 10.1080/09575146.2016.

Matthews, J. (1999) *The Art of Childhood and Adolescence: The Construction of Meaning*. London: Falmer Press.

Mavers, D. (2011) *Children's Drawing and Writing: The Remarkable in the Unremarkable*. Abingdon, Oxon: Routledge.

Mayer, K. (2007) Emerging knowledge about emerging writing. *Young Children*, 62, 34–40.

McInnes, K. (2019) Playful learning in the early years – through the eyes of children. *Education 3–13*, 47 (7), 796–805. DOI: 10.1080/03004279.2019.1622495.

McLachlan, C. J. and Arrow, A. W. (2015) Literacy and the early education curriculum in New Zealand. In W. E. Tunmer and J. W. Chapman (Eds.), *Excellence and Equity in Literacy Education: Palgrave Studies in Excellence and Equity in Global Education.* London: Palgrave Macmillan.

McMahon, S. (2020) *Reconceptualising early language development: matter, sensation and the more-than-human. Discourse: Studies in the Cultural Politics of Education.* DOI: 10.1080/01596306.2020.1767350.

Mercer, N. (1994) Neo-Vygotskian theory and classroom education. In B. Stierer and J. Maybin (Eds.), *Language, Literacy and Learning in Educational Practice* (pp. 92–110). Cambridge: Open University Press.

Merleau-Ponty, M. (2002) *Phenomenology of Perception: An Introduction.* London: Routledge.

Miller, E. B. and Warschauer, M. (2014) Young children and e-reading: Research to date and questions for the future. *Learning, Media and Technology*, 39 (3), 283–305. DOI: 10.1080/17439884.2013.867868.

Ministry of Education, New Zealand (2009) *Oral, Visual, and Written Literacy: Te Kòrero, te Titiro, me te Pànui-Tuhi.* Available online: www.education.govt.nz/assets/Documents/Early-Childhood/Kei-Tua-o-te-Pae/ECEBk17Full.pdf (Accessed 20.04.21).

Ministry of Education, New Zealand (2017) *Te Whāriki: He whariki matauranga mo nga mokopuna o Aotearoa Early Childhood Curriculum.* Available online: education.govt.nz/assets/Documents/Early-Childhood/ELS-Te-Whariki-Early-Childhood-Curriculum-ENG-Web.pdf (Accessed 20.04.21).

Ministry of Education, New Zealand (n.d.) *Te Whāriki online: Language and Literacies.* Available online: tewhariki.tki.org.nz/en/teaching-strategies-and-resources/language-and-literacies/ (Accessed 20.04.21).

Mitton, T. (2017) *Amazing Machines Truckload Children Collection 10 Books Set.* London: Macmillan Books

MODE (2012) *Glossary of Multimodal Terms.* Available online: multimodality-glossary.wordpress.com/(Accessed 20.04.21).

Moedt, K. and Holmes, R. M. (2020) The effects of purposeful play after shared storybook readings on kindergarten children's reading comprehension, creativity, and language skills and abilities. *Early Child Development and Care*, 190 (6), 839–854, DOI: 10.1080/03004430.2018.1496914.

Montessori, M. (1912) *The Montessori Method.* New York: F.A. Stokes.

Montessori. M. (1918) *Spontaneous Activity in Education* (Trans. A. Livingston). London: W. Heinemann.

Montessori, M. (1965) *Dr. Montessori's Own Handbook: A Short Guide to Her Ideas and Materials.* New York: Schocken Books.

Mooney, M. (1990) *Reading To, With, and By Children*. Somers, NY: Richard C Owen Pub.

Moss, P. (2004) *Dedicated to Loris Malaguzzi, The Town of Reggio Emilia and its Schools*. Available online: www.sightlines-initiative.com/images/Library/reggio/townofrepmoss.pdf (Accessed 20.04.21).

Moyles, J. R. (1989) Just Playing? *The Role and Status of Play in Early Childhood Education*. Maidenhead: Open University Press.

Moyles, J. R. (2010) *Thinking about Play: Developing a Reflective Approach*. Maidenhead: Open University Press.

Moyles, J. R. (2014) *The Excellence of Play* (4th ed.). Maidenhead: Open University Press.

Mualem, O. and Klein, P. S. (2013) The communicative characteristics of musical interactions compared with play interactions between mothers and their one-year-old infants. *Early Child Development and Care*, 183 (7), 899–915.

Murray, E. J. and Williams, P. H. (2020) Risk-taking and assessment in toddlers during nature play: The role of family and play context. *Journal of Adventure Education and Outdoor Learning*, 20 (3), 259–273. DOI: 10.1080/14729679.2019.1660193.

Murray, J. (2018) Value/s in early childhood education. *International Journal of Early Years Education*, 26 (3), 215–219. DOI: 10.1080/09669760.2018.1490849.

Mutch, C. and Trim, B. (2013) Improvement, accountability and sustainability: A comparison of developments in the early childhood and schooling sectors. In J. Nuttall (Ed.), *Weaving Te Whāriki – Aotearoa New Zealand's Early Childhood Curriculum Document in Theory and Practice* (2nd ed.). Wellington, New Zealand: NZCER Press.

National Literacy Trust (n.d.) *Early Words Together*. Available online: literacytrust.org.uk/programmes/early-words-together/ (Accessed 20.04.21).

Natural England (2016) *Monitor of Engagement with the Natural Environment: A pilot to develop an indicator of visits to the natural environment by children. Results from years 1 and 2 (March 2013 to February 2015)*. Available online: assets.publishing.service.gov.uk/government/uploads/system/uploads/attachment_data/file/498944/mene-childrens-report-years-1-2.pdf (Accessed 23.04 21).

Neaum, S. (2017) *What Comes Before Phonics*. London: Sage.

Neumann, M. M., Finger, G. and Neumann, D L. (2017) A conceptual framework for emergent digital literacy. *Early Childhood Educational Journal*, 45, 471–479. DOI: 10.1007/s10643-016-0792-z.

New London Group (1996) A pedagogy of multiliteracies: Designing social futures. *Harvard Education Review*, 66 (1), 60–93.

Nicholson, S. (1971) *Theory of Loose Parts: How Not to Cheat Children*. Available online: media.kaboom.org/docs/documents/pdf/ip/Imagination-Playground-Theory-of-Loose-Parts-Simon-Nicholson.pdf (Accessed 29.03.21).

Nicolopoulou, A., Cortina, K. S., Ilgaz, H., Cates, C. B. and de Sá, A. B. (2015) Using a narrative and play-based activity to promote low-income preschoolers' oral language, emergent literacy, and social competence. *Early Childhood Research Quarterly*, 31, 147–162. DOI:10.1016/j.ecresq.

Nicolopoulou, A., McDowell, J. and Brockmeyer, C. (2006) Narrative play and emergent literacy: Storytelling and story-acting meet journal writing. In D. G. Singer, R. M. Golinkoff and K. Hirsh-Pasek (Eds.), *Play = Learning: How Play Motivates and Enhances Children's Cognitive and Social-Emotional Growth* (pp. 124–144). Maidenhead: Open Univeristy Press. DOI:10.1093/acprof:oso/9780195304381.003.0007.

Nicolson, S. and Bracefield, C. (2019) A professional commitment to play. *He Kupu*, 6 (2). Available online: www.hekupu.ac.nz/article/professional-commitment-play (Accessed 20.04.21).

Nikolajeva, M. and Scott, C. (2006) *How Picture Books Work*. London: Routledge.

Ofsted (2017) *Bold Beginnings: The Reception Curriculum in a Sample of Good and Outstanding Primary Schools*. London: DfE. Available online: www.gov.uk/government/publications/reception-curriculum-in-good-and-outstanding-primary-schools-bold-beginnings (Accessed 20.04.21).

PACEY (n.d.) *Mark-making*. Available online: www.pacey.org.uk/mark-making/ (Accessed 20.04.21).

Pahl, K. and Rowsell, J. (2005) *Literacy and Education: Understanding the New Literacy Studies in the Classroom*. London: Paul Chapman Publishing.

Paley, V. G. (1990) *The Boy Who Would be a Helicopter*. Cambridge, MA: Harvard University Press.

Paley, V. G. (1992) *You Can't Say You Can't Play*. Cambridge, MA: Harvard University Press.

Paley, V. G. (2004) *A Child's Work: The Importance of Fantasy Play*. Chicago: University of Chicago Press.

Pellegrini, A. (1984) Identifying casual elements in the thematic–fantasy play paradigm. *American Research Journal*, 21 (3), 691–701.

Pellegrini, A. D. (1985) The relations between symbolic play and literate behavior: A review and critique of the empirical literature. *Review of Educational Research*, 55 (1), 107–121. DOI:10.3102/00346543055001107.

Piaget, J. (1951) *Play, Dreams, and Imitation in Childhood* (Trans. C. Gattegno and F. M. Hodgson). London: Routledge and Kegan Paul, Ltd.

Piaget, J. (1971) *The Science of Education and the Psychology of the Child*. London: Penguin.

Pinker, S. (1994) *The Language Instinct: The New Science of Language and Mind*. London: Allen Lane, the Penguin Press.

Powell, S., Goouch, K. and Werth, L. (2013) *Seeking Froebel's mother songs in daycare for babies*. TACTYC Annual Conference, The ICC Birmingham, UK.

Price, S., Jewitt, C. and Crescenzi, L. (2015) The role of iPads in pre-school children's mark-making development. *Computers & Education*, 87, 131–141. DOI: 10.1016/j.compedu.2015.04.003.

Puranik, C. S. and Lonigan, C. J. (2012) Name-writing proficiency, not length of name, is associated with preschool children's emergent literacy skills. *Early Childhood Research Quarterly*, 27 (2), 284–294. DOI: 10.1016/j.ecresq.2011.09.003.

Pyle, A. and Alaca, B. (2018) Kindergarten children's perspectives on play and learning. *Early Child Development and Care*, 188 (8), 1063–1075. DOI: 10.1080/03004430.2016.1245190.

Qvortrup, J. (2009) Are children human beings or human becomings? A critical assessment of outcome thinking. *Rivista Internazionale di Scienze Sociali*, 3–4, 631–654. Available online: www.jstor.org/stable/41625246 (Accessed 06.04.21).

Rautio, P. and Winston, J. (2015) Things and children in play: Improvisation with language and matter. *Discourse: Studies in the Cultural Politics of Education*, 36 (1), 15–26. DOI: 10.1080/01596306.2013.830806.

Reese, E., Gunn, A., Bateman, A. and Carr, M. (2019) Teacher–child talk about learning stories in New Zealand: A strategy for eliciting children's complex language. *Early Years*, (1–16). DOI: 10.1080/09575146.2019.1621804.

Reggio Children (n.d.) *Exhibitions*. Available online: www.reggiochildren.it/en/exhibitions/ (Accessed 20.04.21).

Reggio Children (n.d.) *Reggio Emilia Approach*. Available online: www.reggiochildren.it/en/reggio-emilia-approach/ (Accessed 20.04.21).

Reggio Children (n.d.) *Values*. Available online: www.reggiochildren.it/en/reggio-emilia-approach/valori-en/ (Accessed 20.04.21).

Richardson, T. and Murray, J. (2017) Are young children's utterances affected by characteristics of their learning environments? A multiple case study. *Early Child Development and Care*, 187 (3–4), 457–468. DOI: 10.1080/03004430.2016.1211116.

Rinaldi, C. (1993) The emergent curriculum and social constructivism. In C. Edwards, L. Gandini and G. Forman (Eds.), *The Hundred Languages of Children: The Reggio Emilia Approach to Early Childhood Education* (pp. 101–111). Norwood, NJ: Ablex.

Rinaldi, C. (2005) *In Dialogue with Reggio Emilia: Listening, Researching and Learning*. Abingdon, Oxon: Routledge.

Ring, K. (2006) Supporting young children drawing: developing a role. *International Journal of Education through Art*, 2 (3), 195–209. DOI: 10.1386/etar.2.3.195_1.

Roberts-Holmes, G. (2014) The 'datafication' of early years pedagogy: 'if the teaching is good, the data should be good and if there's bad teaching, there is bad data'. *Journal of Education Policy*, 30 (3), 302–315. DOI: 10.1080/02680939.2014.924561.

Rogoff, B. (1990) *Apprenticeship in Thinking: Cognitive Development in Social Context*. Oxford: Oxford University Press.

Rose, J. (2005) *Independent Review of the Teaching of Early Reading: Final report*. London: DfES. Available online: dera.ioe.ac.uk/5551/2/report.pdf (Accessed 20.04.21).

Rosen, M. (1993) *We're Going on a Bear Hunt*. London: Walker Books.

Rosen, R. (2017) Play as activism? Early childhood and (inter)generational politics. *Contemporary Social Science*, 12 (1–2), 110–122. DOI: 10.1080/21582041.2017.1324174.

Roskos, K. and Christie, J. (2011) The play–literacy nexus and the importance of evidence-based techniques in the classroom. *American Journal of Play*, 4 (2), 204–224.

Roulstone, S., Law, J., Rush, R., Clegg, J. and Peters, T. (2011) *The Role of Language in Children's Early Educational Outcomes – Research Brief. DFE-RB 134*. Available online: assets.publishing.service.gov.uk/government/uploads/system/uploads/attachment_data/file/181549/DFE-RR134.pdf (Accessed 10.04.21).

Rowe, D. W. (2019) Pointing with a pen: The role of gesture in early childhood writing. *Reading Research Quarterly*, 54 (1), 13–39. DOI: 10.1002/rrq.215.

Sandseter, E. B. H. (2009) *Characteristics of risky play. Journal of Adventure Education and Outdoor Learning*, 9 (1), 3–21. DOI: 10.1080/14729670802702762.

Saracho, O. (2017) Parents' shared storybook reading – learning to read. *Early Child Development and Care*, 187 (3–4), 554–567. DOI:10.1080/03004430.2016.1261514.

Saussure, F. (1966) *Course in General Linguistics*. New York: McGraw-Hill.

Save the Children (2015) *Ready to Read: Closing the gap in early language skills so that every child in England can read well*. Available online: cdn.literacytrust.org.uk/media/documents/Ready_to_Read__-_England_June_2015.pdf (Accessed 10.04.21).

Schiefele, U., Schaffner, E., Möller, J. and Wigfield, A. (2012) Dimensions of reading motivation and their relation to reading behavior and competence. *Reading Research Quarterly*, 47 (4), 427–463. DOI: 10.1002/rrq.030.

Scrafton, E. and Whitington, V. (2015) The accessibility of socio-dramatic play to culturally and linguistically diverse Australian pre-schoolers. *European Early Childhood Education Research Journal*, 23 (2), 213–228. DOI: 10.1080/1350293X.2015.1016806.

Sellers, M. (2012) *Young Children Becoming Curriculum: Deleuze, Te Whāriki and Curricular Understandings*. Abingdon, Oxon: Routledge.

Siraj-Blatchford, I. (2009) Conceptualising progression in the pedagogy of play and sustained shared thinking in early childhood education: A Vygotskian perspective. *Education and Child Psychology*, 26 (2), 77–89.

Skilbeck, A. (2017) Dewey on seriousness, playfulness and the role of the teacher. *Education Sciences*, 7 (16). Available online: files.eric.ed.gov/fulltext/EJ1135035.pdf (Accessed 20.04.21).

Smeed, J. (2012) The grumpy dragon and the angry dragon: From storytelling to storymaking. *Storytelling, Self, Society*, 8, 1–16. DOI: 10.1080/15505340.2012.635092.

Smidt, S. (2006) *The Developing Child in the 21st Century: A Global Perspective on Child Development*. Abingdon, Oxon: Taylor and Francis.

Smidt, S. (2011) *Playing to Learn: The Role of Play in the Early Years*. Abingdon, Oxon: Routledge.

Smidt, S. (2018) *Introducing Trevarthen: A Guide for Practitioners and Students in Early Years Education*. Abingdon, Oxon: Routledge.

Smilansky, S. (1968) *The Effects of Socio-Dramatic Play on Disadvantaged Preschool Children*. New York: Wiley.

Smilansky, S. and Shefataya, L. (1990) *Facilitating Play: A Medium Promoting Cognitive, Socio, Emotional and Academic Development in Young Children*. Gaithersburg, MD: Psychosocial and Educational Publications.

Smith, F. (1992) Learning to read: The never-ending debate. *Phi Delta Kappan*, 74, 432–441.

Smith, K. (2018) *The Playful Writing Project: Exploring playful writing opportunities with reception class teachers*. Available online: www.froebel.org.uk/uploads/documents/Kate-Smith-final-report.pdf (Accessed 20.04.21).

Soler, J. and Miller, L. (2003) The struggle for early childhood curricula: A comparison of the English Foundation Stage Curriculum, Te Whāriki and Reggio Emilia. *International Journal of Early Years Education*, 11 (1), 57–68.

Stagnitti, K. and Lewis F. M. (2015) Quality of pre-school children's pretend play and subsequent development of semantic organization and narrative re-telling skills. *International Journal of Speech-Language Pathology*, 17 (2), 148–158. DOI: 10.3109/17549507.2014.941934.

Stephen, C., Stevenson, O. and Adey, C. (2013) Young children engaging with technologies at home: The influence of family context. *Journal of Early Childhood Research*, 11 (2), 149–164. DOI: 10.1177/1476718X12466215.

Stern, D. N. (1993) The role of feelings for an interpersonal self. In U. Neisser (Ed.), *The Perceived Self: Ecological and Interpersonal Sources of Self-Knowledge* (pp. 205–215). New York: Cambridge University Press.

Stern, D. N. (1999) Vitality contours: The temporal contour of feelings as a basic unit for constructing the infant's social experience. In P. Rochat (Ed.), *Early Social Cognition: Understanding Others in the First Months of Life* (pp. 67–90). Mahwah, NJ: Erlbaum.

Streelansky, J. (2019) A forest-based environment as a site of literacy and meaning making for kindergarten children. *Literacy*, 53 (2), 95–101. DOI: 10.1111/lit.12155.

Street, B. (2001) *Literacy and Development: Ethnographic Perspectives*. London: Routledge.

Street, B. (2013) Literacy in theory and practice: Challenges and debates over 50 years. *Theory Into Practice*, 52, 52–62. DOI: 10.1080/00405841.2013.795442.

Sutton-Smith, B. (1997) *The Ambiguity of Play*. Cambridge, MA: Harvard University Press.

Sylva, K., Siraj-Blatchford, I., Taggert, B., Sammons, P., Elliot, K. and Melhuish, E. (2004) *Project Technical Paper 12 – The Final Report: Effective Preschool Education.* London: DfES and Institute of Education, University of London.

TACTYC (Association for Professional Development in Early Years) (2017) *Bald Beginnings: A Response to Ofsted's (2017) Report, Bold Beginnings: The Reception Curriculum in a Sample of Good and Outstanding Primary Schools. TACTYC.* Available online: tactyc.org.uk/wp-content/uploads/2017/12/Bold-Beginnings-TACTYC-response-FINAL-09.12.17.pdf (Accessed 20.04.21).

Tate (n.d.) *What is Mark-making? Why use Gestural Qualities?* Available online: www.tate.org.uk/art/student-resource/exam-help/mark-making (Accessed 20.04.21).

Teale, W. and Sulzby, E. (1994) Introduction – Emergent literacy as a perspective for examining how young children become writers and readers. In W. Teale and E. Sulzby (Eds.), *Emergent Literacy: Writings and Reading* (6th ed.) (pp. vii–xxv). New Jersey: Ablex Publishing Corporation.

Tickell, C. (2011) *The Early Years: Foundations for Life, Health and Learning – Tickell Review.* Available online: www.education.gov.uk/tickellreview (Accessed 20.04.21).

Tobin, J. (2004) The disappearance of the body in early childhood education. In L. Bresler (Ed.), *Knowing Bodies, Knowing Mind: Towards Embodied Teaching and Learning* (pp. 111–125). Dordrecht, The Netherlands: Kluwer Academic.

Torgerson, C., Brooks, G., Gascoine, L. and Higgins, S. (2019) Phonics: Reading policy and the evidence of effectiveness from a systematic 'tertiary' review. *Research Papers in Education*, 34 (2), 208–238. DOI: 10.1080/02671522.2017.1420816.

Toub, T. S., Hassinger-Das, B., Nesbitt, K. T., Ilgaz, H., Skolnick Weisberga, D., Hirsh-Paseka, K., Michnick Golinkoff, R., Nicolopouloud, A. and Dickinson, D. K. (2018) The language of play: Developing preschool vocabulary through play following shared book-reading. *Early Childhood Research Quarterly*, 45, 1–17. DOI: 10.1016/j.ecresq.2018.01.010.

Tovey, H. (2007) *Playing Outdoors: Spaces and Places, Risk and Challenge.* Maidenhead: Open University Press.

Tovey, H. (2013) *Bringing the Froebel Approach to your Early Years Practice.* Abingdon, Oxon: Routledge.

Tovey, H. (2017) *Outdoor Play and Exploration.* Available online: www.froebel.org.uk/training-and-resources/pamphlets (Accessed 20.03.21).

Trehub, S. E., Ghazban, N. and Corbeil, M. (2015) Musical affect regulation in infancy. *Annals of the New York Academy of Sciences*, 1337 (1), 186–192.

Trevarthen, C. (1999) Musicality and the intrinsic motive pulse: Evidence from human psychobiology and infant communication. *Musicae Scientiae: Rhythm, Musical Narrative and Origins of Human Communication* (pp.157–213). Liege, Belgium: European Society for the Cognitive Sciences of Music.

Trevarthen, C. (2005) 'Stepping away from the mirror: Pride and shame in adventures of companionship' – Reflections on the nature and emotional needs of infant intersubjectivity. In C. S. Carter, L. Ahnert, K. E. Grossmann, S. B. Hardy,

M. E. Lamb, S. W. Porges and N. Sachser (Eds.), *Attachment and Bonding: A New Synthesis* (pp. 55–84). New York: MIT.

Undheim, M. and Jernes, M. (2020) Teachers' pedagogical strategies when creating digital stories with young children. *European Early Childhood Education Research Journal*, 28 (2), 256–271. DOI: 10.1080/1350293X.2020.1735743.

UNICEF (1989) *The United Nations Convention on the Rights of the Child.* Available online: www.unicef.org.uk/what-we-do/un-convention-child-rights/ (Accessed 10.04.21).

UNICEF (2019) *Digital Literacy for Children: Exploring Definitions and Frameworks.* Available online: www.unicef.org/globalinsight/media/1271/file/%20UNICEF-Global-Insight-digital-literacy-scoping-paper-2020.pdf (Accessed 20.04.21).

University of York (n.d.) *BabyLab Studies: Research in Phonological Development: How do Babies Learn to Talk?* Available online: www.york.ac.uk/language/research/projects/babylab/ Accessed (20.04.21).

Vecchi, V. (2010) *Art and Creativity in Reggio Emilia: Exploring the Role and Potential of Ateliers in Early Childhood Education.* London: Routledge.

Venn, L. (2014) *Family Reading Habits and the Impact of Bookstart: Executive Summary of Findings. BookTrust.* Available online: www.booktrust.org.uk/globalassets/resources/research/bookstart-evaluation-executive-summary-final.pdf (Accessed 20.04.21).

Vidal-Hall, C., Flewitt, R. and Wyse, D. (2020) Early childhood practitioner beliefs about digital media: Integrating technology into a child-centred classroom environment. *European Early Childhood Education Research Journal*, 28 (2), 167–181. DOI: 10.1080/1350293X.2020.1735727.

Vulchanova, M., Baggio, G., Cangelosi, A. and Smith, L. (2017) Editorial: Language development in the digital age. *Frontiers in Human Neuroscience*, 11, 447. DOI: 10.3389/fnhum.2017.00447.

Vuorikari, R., Punie, Y., Carretero, G. and Van den Brande, G. (2016) *DigComp 2.0: The Digital Competence Framework for Citizens.* Available online: ec.europa.eu/jrc/en/publication/eur-scientific-and-technical-research-reports/digcomp-20-digital-competence-framework-citizens-update-phase-1-conceptual-reference-model (Accessed 20.04.21).

Vygotsky, L. S. (1967) Play and its role in the mental development of the child. *Soviet Psychology*, 5 (3), 6–18. DOI: 10.2753/RPO1061-040505036.

Vygotsky, L. S. (1978) *Mind in Society: Development in Higher Psychological Process.* Cambridge MA: Harvard University Press.

Vygotsky, L. S. (1986) *Thought and Language.* Cambridge, MA: MIT Press.

Vygotsky, L. S. (1997) *The Collected Works of L. S. Vygotsky: Vol. 4. The History of the Development of Higher Mental Functions* (Trans. M. J. Hall (R. W. Rieber Ed.)). New York: Plenum.

Vygotsky. L. S. (2004) Imagination and creativity in childhood. *Journal of Russian & East European Psychology*, 42 (1), 7–97, DOI: 10.1080/10610405.2004.11059210.

Waite, S. (2020) Where are we going? International views on purposes, practices and barriers in school-based outdoor learning. *Education Science*, 10 (11), 311. DOI: 10.3390/educsci10110311.

Weisberg, D. S., Zosh, J. M., Hirsh-Pasek, K. and Golinkoff, R. M. (2013) Talking it up: Play, language development, and the role of adult support. *American Journal of Play*, 6 (1), 39–54.

Wells, K. (2009) *Childhood in Global Perspective*. Cambridge: Polity Press.

Whitebread, D. (2012) *The Importance of Play: A Report on the Value of Children's Play with a Series of Policy Recommendations. Toy Industries Europe (TIE)*. Available online: http://www.csap.cam.ac.uk/media/uploads/files/1/david-whitebread—importance-of-play-report.pdf (Accessed 20.04.21).

Whitehead, M. (2007) *Developing Language and Literacy with Young Children*. London: Sage.

Wohlwend, K. E. (2008) Research directions: Play as a literacy of possibilities: Expanding meanings in practices, materials, and spaces. *Language Arts*, 86 (2), 127–136.

Wohlwend, K. E. (2011) *Playing their Way into Literacies: Reading, Writing, and Belonging in the Early Childhood Classroom*. New York: Teacher College Press.

Wohlwend, K. E. (2013) *Literacy Playshop: New Literacies, Popular Media, and Play in the Early Childhood Classroom*. New York: Teacher College Press.

Wohlwend, K. E. (2017) Who gets to play? Access, popular media and participatory literacies. *Early Years*, 37 (1), 62–76. DOI: 10.1080/09575146.2016.1219699.

Wohlwend, K. E. (2018) Play as the literacy of children: Imagining otherwise in contemporary childhoods. In D. E. Alvermann, N. J. Unrau and M. Sailors (Eds.), *Theoretical Models and Processes of Literacy* (7th ed., pp. 301–318). New York: Routledge.

Wood, C., Vardy, E. and Tarczynski-Bowles, L. (2015) *Final Report – Early Words Together: Impact on Families and Children*. Available online: files.eric.ed.gov/fulltext/ED560649.pdf (Accessed 20.04.21).

Wood, E. (2010) Reconceptualising the play–pedagogy relationship. In L. Brooker and S. Edwards (Eds.), *Engaging Play* (pp. 11–24). Maidenhead: Open University Press.

Wood. E. and Attfield, J. (2005) *Play, Learning and the Early Childhood Curriculum*. London: Sage.

Wyse, D. and Goswami, U. (2008) Synthetic phonics and the teaching of reading. *British Educational Research Journal*, 34 (6), 691–710. DOI: 10.1080/01411920802268912.

Yamada-Rice, D. (2013) The semiotic landscape and three-year-olds' emerging understanding of multimodal communicative practices. *Journal of Early Childhood Literacy*, 12 (2), 154–184. DOI: 10.1177/1476718X12463913.

Young, M. (2014) What is a curriculum and what can it do? *The Curriculum Journal*, 25 (1), 7–13. DOI: 10.1080/09585176.2014.902526.

Zevenbergen, A. A. and Whitehurst, G. J. (2003) Dialogic reading: A shared picture book reading intervention for preschoolers. In A. van Kleeck, S. A. Stahl and E. B. Bauer (Eds.), *On Reading Books to Children: Parents and Teachers* (pp. 177–200). Mahwah, NJ: Lawrence Erlbaum Associates Publishers.

INDEX